Why Are We So CLUELESS about the STOCK MARKET?

Learn how to invest your money, how to pick stocks, and how to make money in the stock market

MARIUSZ SKONIECZNY

CLASSIC VALUE INVESTORS LLC

Why Are We So CLUELESS about the Stock Market?

Learn how to invest your money,
how to pick stocks, and
how to make money in the stock market

Written by
Mariusz Skonieczny

Investment Publishing
Schaumburg, IL

Printed by Investment Publishing
Schaumburg, IL

Copyright © 2009 by Mariusz Skonieczny

First printing 2009
Printed in the United States of America

12 11 10 09

ISBN 978-0-615-28748-5
LCCN: 2009927916

Cover design and interior page layout by Kerrie Lian, under contract with MacGraphics Services.

TABLE OF CONTENTS

PREFACE

I was inspired to write this book by the 2008-09 economic recession that started with the bust in the housing market. The Dow Jones Industrial Average fell from its high of approximately 14,000 in July 2007 to about 6,500 in March 2009. The majority of people who were invested in the stock market saw their 401(k)s, IRAs, or other investment accounts decline 50% or more.

During the same period, my investment portfolio lost nothing. As a matter of fact, it showed a gain of 5.81% in 2008 and 75.49% during the first five months of 2009. I only had 10 stocks in my portfolio, and one of my stocks quadrupled, two doubled, and the rest showed gains anywhere between 9% and 89%.

Why did I achieve this performance when everyone else experienced investment losses? Is the answer that I am some kind of a stock market genius or hold a PhD in economics? No, neither of these descriptions is the reason. The answer lies in the fact that I was almost 100% in cash before the market started collapsing. When analyzing stocks in 2007 and early 2008, I was not able to find anything trading at reasonable prices. Staying in cash was the best alternative.

As I later realized, I was not the only one having this problem. Warren Buffett was not buying much during the same period but was just accumulating cash. He was criticized for doing so because some wanted him to invest it and others wanted him to return it to Berkshire Hathaway's shareholders in the form of dividends. Like Mr. Buffett, I patiently waited for opportunities.

When the stock market crashed, the opportunities to buy excellent companies were plentiful. The companies, such as American Express and Wells Fargo, which I had dreamed of owning for years, became available at prices well below their values.

So how come most mutual funds, financial advisors, and other money managers failed to see the lack of investment opportunities during the peak in 2007 and early 2008? Maybe some of them did, but even so, they would have failed to act because of the compensation system that was in place. The majority of money managers are paid a percentage of assets under management. For example, if the assets under management are $100 million and the management fee is 1.5%, the money manager will receive $1.5 million (1.5% x $100 million). Under this compensation system, generating above-average returns and protecting investors' money is secondary. The primary concern for these managers is to have as much assets under management as possible and to be fully invested at all times. How likely is it for a money manager making $1.5 million in fees to go 100% cash when he or she is supposed to be investing the money, not sitting on cash? If a money manager did go 100% cash, he or she would have been criticized as Warren Buffett was criticized for having too much cash. Going cash or returning the money to the investors would be equivalent to quitting a $1.5 million job.

So what could the individual investors have done to prevent themselves from seeing their portfolios lose half of their values within a matter of months? Since investment professionals and other so called experts may not always act in their clients' best interests, there is only one option left: do it yourself. But the problem is that the majority of the general public does not have enough knowledge to take it upon themselves. To illustrate my point, let me pose this question:

> *What did the general public do when the 2008-09 recession provided 1-in-a-100-years investment opportunities?*

Many panicked and sold their holdings by cashing in their retirement plans or other investment accounts. The investors who did not sell kept sitting on the same stocks that had lost money. If an investor's portfolio went from $100,000 to $50,000, in order to break even the $50,000 portfolio would have to double. However, it might not be realistic to break even with the same set of stocks. An investor in this situation should ask himself or herself,

If I had $50,000 in cash would I still invest in the stocks that I currently hold?

If the answer is no, the funds should be placed somewhere else where there is a greater potential for growth. If on December 31, 2008, the above investor had invested this $50,000 in stocks that were in my portfolio, it would have grown to about $87,745 by the end of the fifth month of 2009.

The panicky and fearful behavior of many individual investors is indicative of how unprepared and uninformed we as a society are about investing. It has been my experience that most people lack basic investment knowledge, but because some of us are successful in our careers, we assume that we will be good at investing. Nothing can be further from the truth. For example, doctors are notorious for making poor investment decisions.

Why Are We So Clueless About the Stock Market?

Because we

- panic and run away when the stock market is serving us unbelievable deals,
- jump on the wagon or stay in the wagon when the market is overpriced,
- do not understand the difference between stocks and businesses,
- do not know how businesses make investors wealthy,
- cannot differentiate between excellent and mediocre businesses,
- do not know how to value stocks,
- do not realize how over-diversification can destroy returns, and
- do not understand why investing in IPOs is not a good idea.

In this book readers will learn to identify the missing pieces of the puzzle in investment strategies and the way to arrange them in order to realize investment success. The fundamentals presented will decrease the chances of making investment mistakes, and most importantly, will make us think twice about whether we are investing or simply gambling and calling it investing.

Mariusz Skonieczny

ACKNOWLEDGMENTS

I am grateful to all the individuals who helped me with the book. First, I would like to thank my editors C. Daniel Miller and Joyce L. Miller of Integrated Writer Services. I cannot overemphasize the importance of their contribution to making this book a reality. Second, I would like to thank Karen Saunders of MacGraphics Services and Kerrie Lian for the design of the book cover and interior. Thanks go to Tom Fitzgerald for his assistance with the figures throughout the book. Finally, but not least, I would like to thank the following people for reading the original manuscript and providing me their valuable feedback: Roger Dabdab, Barbara Jester, David Jester, Mary Jester, Kathleen Nate, and Jason VanDevelde.

Chapter 1

STOCKS VERSUS BUSINESSES

STOCKS VERSUS BUSINESSES

Although there is so much information available about intelligent investing, the general public has a limited understanding of investment basics. When people think of the stock market, they see ticker symbols moving across computer screens. Investment professionals and the media often make the subject of investing overly complicated. It may be easier for money managers to obtain clients when they confuse them and make them believe that investing is only for rocket scientists.

Investors should understand the difference between stocks and businesses. Stocks are certificates of ownership in particular businesses and cannot exist without these underlying businesses. Businesses, on the other hand, are enterprises whose purpose is to manufacture products or provide services for compensation.

How Do Businesses Come into Existence?

In the interest of simplicity, let's look at a business that is easy to understand. Tom, an entrepreneur, wants to use his grandmother's lemonade recipe to open a lemonade stand. If he sells enough lemonade, he will earn an adequate return on his investment.

Tom has $1,000, which is his original equity. To launch his business, he will need the following:

1) $100 for ingredients – inventory
2) $300 for tools – equipment
3) $0 for place of production – Tom's house
4) $400 for a cart – equipment
5) $100 for cups – inventory

After spending $900 for equipment and inventory, he is left with $100 in cash. Every business needs some cash to operate. Tom's business will have the following balance sheet.

Fig. 1: Year 1 Balance Sheet

Tom's Lemonade Enterprise Balance Sheet	
ASSETS	
Cash	$100
Inventory	$200
Equipment	$700
TOTAL ASSETS	$1,000
LIABILITIES	$0
OWNER'S EQUITY	$1,000
TOTAL LIABILITIES & OWNERS EQUITY	$1,000

Note: Assets must equal Liabilities + Owner's Equity. Because Tom used his own money, he does not have any liabilities.

If Tom had left his money in a savings account at the bank instead, he would have earned 2%, or $20 per year, on his money ($1,000 x 2% = $20). He needs to generate more than $20 per year of net income from his business in order to earn better returns than the bank provides.

Tom believes he can make $100 per year operating his business. Because his equity, shown in the balance sheet above, is $1,000, he will need to earn 10% on his investment. This is equivalent to a *Return on Equity* (ROE) of 10%.

Return on Equity = Net Income/Equity

A 10% return from his business is much better than a 2% return from the bank. In order to see if Tom can achieve this return, we need to examine his revenues and expenses.

During the first year of operations, he sold $800 worth of lemonade, and spent $700 to operate his business. Tom's estimation was correct because he earned a net income of $100. His income statement is shown in Figure 2.

Fig. 2: Year 1 Income Statement

Tom's Lemonade Enterprise Income Statement	
Revenue	
Lemonade Sales	$800
Expenses	
Cost of Ingredients	$100
Cost of Cups	$100
Wages *	$300
Rent for the Stand	$200
Total Expenses	$700
Net Income	$100

Note: Wages are included. If Tom hires someone to make and sell lemonade, he will have to pay wages. If Tom decides to make and sell lemonade himself, he will pay himself wages because he could spend his time somewhere else and get paid $300 for his time. Because he is also the owner of the company, he will collect the net income in addition to wages.

Tom's Lemonade Enterprises only has one owner. The business produced a net income of $100 in the first year of operation. This income attaches value to the business. Thus, he could technically sell his entire business, or part of it, to one individual, many individuals, or the general public through an *Initial Public Offering (IPO)*.

> **IPO — An *Initial Public Offering* is a process that private companies use to sell part or all of a business to investors. As part of the IPO, the shares begin trading on stock exchanges.**

If Tom does sell his business to the public, investors can buy shares of his business and have a small percentage of ownership in his enterprise. If the IPO were offered to a total of 100 investors, the $100 of net income would belong to those investors. Each share would be assigned $1.00 ($100 net income/100 investors). Over the long term, the value of the shares is directly correlated with earnings assigned to each share, just as a private business is worth more when it generates more money. In the short term, price and value might not correlate, but in the end, the price that investors are willing to pay for a share will depend on how much the company's earnings will be.

Conclusion

The most important concept presented in this chapter is that stocks are a way to be an owner of a company. If a business performs well over time, its stock price will appreciate to reflect the value of the underlying business.

Chapter 2

HOW DO BUSINESSES MAKE INVESTORS WEALTHY?

HOW DO BUSINESSES MAKE INVESTORS WEALTHY?

In our previous example, Tom invested $1,000 into his business, and in the first year of operation, his Return on Equity was 10%. This obviously is better than the 2% return on his savings account with the bank.

Tom now has $100 generated by his business. Assuming he does not want to sell his business, what should he do? Some of his options are as follows:

1) put the $100 in the bank and keep operating his business or
2) reinvest the $100 in his business.

Option 1

Under the first option, Tom can put $100 in the bank and keep operating his business. The bank will only pay 2% interest, which is a return of $2 per year. As an entrepreneur, Tom is not satisfied with a 2% return.

Option 2

If Tom chooses to reinvest the $100 back into the business, he can use the money to increase revenues or decrease expenses. Either one would improve the value of his business by increasing the net income. To reduce operating expenses, Tom could upgrade his equipment so that the business is more efficient. To increase revenue, Tom could sell more lemonade, increase the price of lemonade, or open another stand. Tom chooses to increase revenues by opening another stand.

It cost him $1,000 to open his first stand. He only has $100. However, he does not need to spend the same amount of money to open the second stand because he can continue to use the same location and equipment to produce lemonade for both stands. Therefore, he can open the second stand for $700 ($400 for a cart, $200 for ingredients and cups, and $100 in cash for working capital). Where is the additional $600 going to come from?

In order to cover the difference, he applies for a $600 bank loan, and a loan officer reviews Tom's Lemonade Enterprise's balance sheet (Fig. 1) and income statement (Fig. 2). After analyzing the financials, the loan officer offers Tom a $600 loan at 7% interest. Tom knows that his business can produce 10% return on investment, so he can afford an interest rate of 7%. The new balance sheet, including the $600 loan, is shown in Figure 3.

Fig. 3: Year 2 Balance Sheet

Tom's Lemonade Enterprise Balance Sheet	
Assets	
Cash ($100 + $100)	$200
Inventory ($200 + $200)	$400
Equipment ($700 + $400)	$1,100
Total Assets	**$1,700**
Liabilities	
Bank Loan	$600
Total Liabilities	$600
Owner's Equity *	$1,100
Total Liabilities & Owner's Equity	**$1,700**

Note: Tom's equity is $1,100, which is equal to his original $1,000 plus $100 net income from operating his business the first year.

Assuming that both stands will have results identical to those produced by the first stand during its first year of operation, his income statement for Year 2 is shown in Figure 4.

Fig. 4: Year 2 Income Statement

Tom's Lemonade Enterprise Income Statement	
Revenue	
Lemonade Sales ($800 x 2)	$1,600
Expenses	
Cost of Ingredients ($100 x 2)	$200
Cost of Cups ($100 x 2)	$200
Wages ($300 x 2)	$600
Rent for the Stand ($200 x 2)	$400
Interest Expense ($600 x 7%)*	**$42**
Total Expenses	$1,442
Net Income	**$158**

Note: Interest Expense is included.

What is his return on equity? The formula for return on equity, as mentioned before, is net income divided by equity. In this case, the formula for Year 2 return on equity is Year 2 net income ($158) divided by Year 2 equity ($1,100) or $158/$1,100 = 14.36%. The return on equity increased from 10% in Year 1 to 14.36% in Year 2 because of the leverage created by debt. Return on equity is discussed in more detail later in this book.

Competition Enters the Market

Following one year of operating two stands, Tom faces a dilemma of what to do with his $158 of newly generated income. Because he was able to earn high returns over the past two years, competitors notice how successful his lemonade business has been, and they try to copy it and undercut his prices.

If Tom loses some business to his competitors, he either will sell less lemonade or be forced to cut his prices to keep his market share. In either case, he will not be able to keep earnings at the same level as in previous years. Because of new competition, Tom keeps $158 in cash in case competitors take too much of his business. He wants to have enough liquidity to stay afloat and be able to pay the interest on his bank loan.

If Tom loses 15% of his revenue to competitors in Year 3, his income statement will look like the one in Figure 5 below.

Fig. 5: Year 3 Income Statement

Tom's Lemonade Enterprise Income Statement	
Revenue	
Lemonade Sales ($1,600 x 85%)	$1,360
Expenses	
Cost of Ingredients ($200 x 85%)	$170
Cost of Cups ($200 x 85%)	$170
Wages	$600
Rent for the Stand	$400
Interest Expense ($600 x 7%)	$42
Total Expenses	$1,382
Net Income	**-$22**

A comparison of Figures 4 and 5 shows that the revenue in Year 3 is reduced by 15% from $1,600 in Year 2 to $1,360 in Year 3. Note that his expenses are also reduced from $1,442 to $1,382 because the costs of ingredients and cups are reduced. They are variable costs that fluctuate with volume. Wages, rent, and the interest on his loan are fixed and have to be paid regardless of the revenue earned. Laying off employees could decrease wages, but because Tom has to have someone operating both stands, wages remain unchanged.

After losing 15% of his business to competitors, Tom's Lemonade Enterprise generates a loss of $22 in Year 3. Now his returns are negative. Tom is frustrated because he originally invested $1,000 to open his business, which generated $100, $158, and -$22 in Years 1, 2, and 3 respectively. He worked hard to make his returns, and now, as a result of competition, he might never again achieve high enough returns to make his business venture worthwhile.

What factors in this scenario could be altered in order to achieve positive returns?

Competition Enters the Market but Tom's Business Is Protected

If Tom generates attractive returns, it is inevitable that competition will enter the market. But in an alternate scenario, Tom does not sell ordinary lemonade. He sells a special recipe with a distinctive taste. Tom gives it a brand name of "Lemonade Special." Customers love it so much that they pay Tom's price even if other competitors sell lemonade at lower prices.

Because of this special taste and distinctive brand name, Tom's revenues are protected from competition, and he is able to maintain his market share and prices. This kind of protection is called a *moat* or a *competitive advantage*.

> **A moat** is a competitive advantage that protects a company's profits from its competitors in the same way a moat protected a castle from invaders. The term was coined by Warren Buffett.

But Why Does it Matter?

The main goal of this chapter is to answer the question, "How do businesses make investors wealthy?" Tom started with $1,000 that he invested to generate a net income of $100 in Year 1. He invested $100 of net income and $600 of debt to generate a net income of $158 in Year 2. The value of his business was higher in Year 2 because his business earned more money. The value depends on several factors such as whether the net income will keep growing and the certainty of the income stream. A more detailed discussion of valuation is covered later in this book.

If Tom's business stops growing and generates $158 every year, it will still have value. To determine this value, it is necessary to estimate how much a potential buyer would be willing to pay for his business. But what exactly would the buyer be buying? The buyer would be buying an expected income stream of $158 per year. The price the buyer is willing to pay will also depend on what rate of return the buyer would require. Since anyone can achieve a return of 2% at the banks with virtually no risk, the rate of return would have to be higher than that in order to make it worthwhile for an investor or buyer.

Let us assume that a buyer would require a 10% rate of return. The buyer would be willing to pay as much as $1,580 to achieve that return. It is calculated by taking $158 divided by 10% or 0.10. In other words, the buyer would invest $1,580 to get $158 every year. The buyer's return would be 10% ($158/$1,580).

If Tom sold the business for $1,580 at the end of Year 2, he would net $580 because originally he invested $1,000 to start the business. This would be equivalent to a return of 58% over the two years. If he kept his money in the bank instead of opening a business, he would have $1,040 because the rate of return would be approximately 2%.

A return of 58% over a two-year period is equivalent to a return of 25.70% annually. To understand how we arrived at this figure, one needs to understand the concept of compounding, which is explained in the chapter on valuation. What if Tom does not sell his business and because of its competitive advantage, it keeps growing his net worth of $1,000 at 25.70% per year for the next 20 years?

Growing Tom's initial $1,000 investment at 25.70% per year each year will result in $96,985 in 20 years, as Figure 6 illustrates. That's more than 96 times the original amount. This is the power of compounding, and that's how great businesses make investors wealthy. As businesses increase earnings and reinvest them at high rates of return, those newly generated earnings make the businesses more valuable.

Fig. 6: Compounding Net Worth

Year	Net Worth
0	$1,000
1	$1,257
2	$1,580
3	$1,986
4	$2,497
5	$3,138
6	$3,945
7	$4,958
8	$6,233
9	$7,835
10	$9,848
11	$12,379
12	$15,560
13	$19,560
14	$24,586
15	$30,905
16	$38,848
17	$48,831
18	$61,381
19	$77,156
20	$96,985

How can other investors, such as those in the general public, grow wealth? Investors can become owners by purchasing shares in Tom's business or any other enterprise available for sale. Because Tom's business is a private business, let's take it public to illustrate how individual investors can benefit from the wealth growth.

Taking it Public

To take the company public, Tom's business has to go through an Initial Public Offering. Once the company becomes public, its shares start trading on national exchanges such as the New York Stock Exchange or NASDAQ (National Association of Securities Dealers Automated Quotations).

Let's assume that Tom wants to take 100% of his business public after Year 2. The financials for Year 2 are shown below in Figures 7 and 8. Notice that they are the same as Figures 3 and 4.

Fig. 7: Balance Sheet for Year 2

Tom's Lemonade Enterprise Balance Sheet	
Assets	
Cash ($100 + $100)	$200
Inventory ($200 + $200)	$400
Equipment ($700 + $400)	$1,100
Total Assets	**$1,700**
Liabilities	
Bank Loan	$600
Total Liabilities	$600
Owner's Equity	$1,100
Total Liabilities & Owner's Equity	**$1,700**

Fig. 8: Income Statement for Year 2

Tom's Lemonade Enterprise Income Statement	
Revenue	
Lemonade Sales ($800 x 2)	$1,600
Expenses	
Cost of Ingredients ($100 x 2)	$200
Cost of Cups ($100 x 2)	$200
Wages ($300 x 2)	$600
Rent for the Stand ($200 x 2)	$400
Interest Expense ($600 x 7%)	$42
Total Expenses	$1,442
Net Income	**$158**

When Tom hires investment bankers to help him take the company public, they inform him that the business can be sold for $2,370. Investment bankers assume that the earnings will keep growing instead of being flat from year to year. Therefore, they price it higher than what we previously demonstrated. What is important to understand is that if the earnings are expected to grow, the buyer will be willing to pay more for the business than if the earnings are expected to remain the same. Valuation is discussed in more detail later. For now, assume that $2,370 is a fair price. Investment banking fees have been omitted for simplicity. The company issues 100 shares, and each share is purchased for $23.70 ($2,370/100). Also, each share is assigned a part of net income. In our case, the net income is $158 and there are 100 shares; therefore, annual *earnings per share* are $1.58. The *price to earnings ratio* (P/E ratio) is 15 ($23.70/$1.58).

P/E Ratio = Price per Share/Earnings per Share

Tom takes his $2,370 and moves on to other investment alternatives.

The Company is Public — How Can It Grow Wealth?

When the company's management decides to open new lemonade stands, pay down debt, or improve efficiency, it is making *capital allocation* decisions on behalf of the owners.

Aside from the day-to-day operations of the business, it is the management's responsibility to allocate capital properly to grow value for the shareholders. Capital can come from different sources to finance operations and can be classified as either liability or equity. It can be generated internally in the form of earnings, or it can come from sources outside the business such as from creditors or other investors. Internally generated earnings can be

1. reinvested to maintain the firm's productive infrastructure,
2. returned to shareholders in the form of dividends,
3. used for share buybacks,
4. used to pay down debt,
5. reinvested in the business, and
6. used to acquire other businesses.

Maintaining Firm's Productivity

Before a company can distribute its earnings, it must first spend a portion needed to maintain its productivity level. Railroad companies, for example, have to spend significantly more on maintaining their infrastructure than companies in less capital-intensive industries. Companies that do not need to spend a significant amount of money on maintaining productivity levels have more money remaining for other activities that grow earnings instead of just maintaining them.

Dividends

Companies may pay out a portion of their earnings in cash dividends. However, when companies are expanding quickly, investors are better served if the management reinvests the earnings back into the business instead of paying them out as dividends. Mature companies, such as Coca-Cola and General Electric, are more likely to pay out a significant portion of earnings with dividends because they have limited growth opportunities in relation to their sizes. Shareholders benefit from dividends because they can either spend them or reinvest them by buying more shares of the same company or other companies.

Share Repurchases

Another way that companies can benefit shareholders is by buying back their own shares. Figure 9 is an illustration of how $5.00 of earnings is distributed among five shareholders.

Fig. 9: $5.00 Distributed Among Five Shareholders

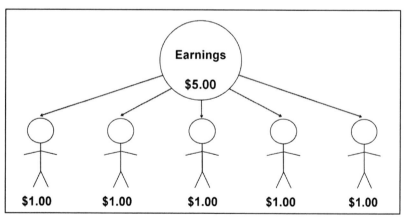

When a company's management buys back shares, they are buying out some of the company's shareholders. The remaining shareholders get a bigger share of earnings as illustrated in Figure 10.

Fig. 10: $5.00 Distributed Among Four Shareholders

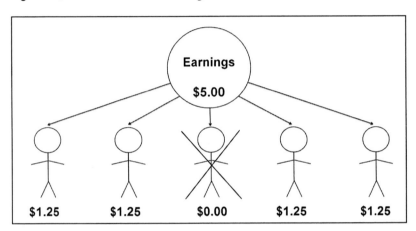

Even though the earnings for the company as a whole stayed at $5.00, the company benefited shareholders because *earnings per share* increased from $1.00 to $1.25. The value of individual shares increased as a result of the repurchase. Whether this was a good decision or not depends on whether the money used to repurchase shares could have been more valuably used to grow the company's earnings.

Capital is allocated most efficiently when a company repurchases its own shares when a stock is undervalued. Capital is wasted when a company purchases its own shares when they are overpriced. Assuming the value of each stock above is $15, is it better to buy out the center shareholder for $50 or for $5? If an investor is one of the remaining shareholders, he or she should want the management to pay out the center shareholder for $5 instead of $50. If the management is willing to pay $50, an investor should want to be the center shareholder because he or she would be getting more money for his or her share than it is worth!

Repurchasing shares at overpriced levels is not a good use of capital, but it is even worse when a company borrows money to make share repurchases of overpriced securities. If a company cannot generate enough funds internally, it should not be engaging in share repurchases.

Reduction of Debt

A company may use some of its earnings to pay down debt. This reduces interest expense and makes the company less vulnerable to economic slowdowns. The downside is that it limits expansion potential.

Reinvestment in the Business

A company may reinvest its earnings back into itself and grow earnings. This reinvestment may include spending money on research and development, new products or services, new factories or equipment, and hiring employees. When a company reinvests in itself, it is growing internally. *Internal growth* is generally preferred to *external growth* (discussed in the next point) because it is usually cheaper. Newer companies rarely pay dividends or make share repurchases because of the abundance of investment opportunities that allow capital to be allocated at high returns on investments.

Acquisitions

Finally, earnings may be used for acquisitions of other businesses. This is referred to as *external growth*. Companies may make acquisitions for good reasons such as diversification of products or increased geographic coverage. However, acquisitions can be abused. A CEO in pursuit of prestige and fame that comes with the size of the firm may engage in numerous acquisitions per year. Oftentimes, companies overpay for the acquisitions and waste capital in the process.

The internal growth of every company slows down after a company matures. Those who find it hard to accept the deceleration may seek acquisitions as a cure. Growing through acquisitions may mean buying growth at high prices while shareholders pay the bill. Acquisitions are often pricey because companies typically pay premiums to acquire control of the target companies. Individual investors buying small portions of businesses can obtain better prices because they are not taking control of the acquired businesses.

Acquisitions may also dilute the moat that surrounds a specific business unit. For example, Moody's Investors Services has a moat that protects its credit rating business. Wells Fargo has a moat that protects its banking operations. It does not make much sense for any company to acquire non-moat businesses that have no connection to their core businesses.

Conclusion

Excellent companies with competent management that effectively reinvest capital at high rates are able to grow wealth for investors. Buying these businesses is one of the best ways for investors to put their money to work. The next chapter explores what constitutes a good business.

Chapter 3

WHAT IS A GOOD BUSINESS?

WHAT IS A GOOD BUSINESS?

What is a good business? One way to think about it is to imagine a machine that takes money in on the left and puts money out on the right. Some businesses are able to deliver more on the right than other businesses. In the illustration in Figure 11, we have an exceptional business that is able to produce $1.30 for every $1.00 it consumes.

Fig. 11: Excellent Business

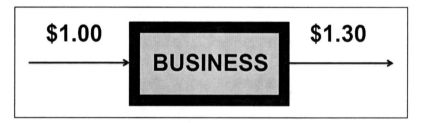

If it takes one year for the money to go through this process, $10,000 consumed during the year will produce an outcome of $13,000 by the end of the year. The newly generated $13,000 can then be reinserted on the left, and a year later 30% more will be generated on the right. If the process is repeated for 30 years, $10,000 will grow into $26,199,956. That would mean that a person who is 30 years old could set aside a one-time sum of $10,000 for 30 years and not worry about retirement. In another scenario, parents could set aside $1,000 for their child's college education the day their child is born. After 18 years, this $1,000 would grow into $112,455.

Figure 12 illustrates examples of three businesses: Business A, B, and C. If all other factors are equal, it is obvious which business is the most productive.

Fig. 12: Businesses A, B, and C

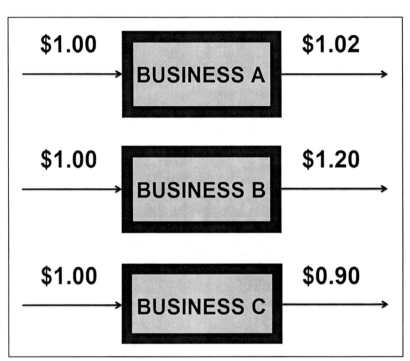

Business A takes in $1.00 and produces $1.02, which is a 2% return. A savings account at a bank offers the same return with no risk because all deposits up to a certain amount are insured by the FDIC (Federal Deposit Insurance Corporation). Therefore, there is no reason to own a business such as this one. Business B takes in $1.00 and generates $1.20 – a 20% return. While not as appealing as the 30% return in the previous example, it is still an excellent return. Business C takes in $1.00 and produces $0.90. This is a negative 10% return. Every time money is inserted on the left, less is produced on the right. The original $1.00 investment would eventually reach $0 if invested in Business C. If Business B clearly is the best of the three, why would anyone ever invest in a business such as Business A, or even worse, one such as Business C? However, investors do it all the time.

In 1997, General Motors' *earnings per share* (EPS) were $7.89, according to the Value Line Investment Survey. In 2006, earnings per share were at $3.89, and in 2007, they were -$0.33. Based on only the EPS, this does not appear to be a good investment. But what about the stock price? In 1997, GM stock was trading at $72. In February 2009, it was trading for approximately $2. Owning GM would have been a terrible investment if it had been purchased at $72 and held until February 2009. But would it be a good investment to buy it at $2 because it is so low? If it is purchased at $2 and it increases to $72, the investment return would be 3,500%. However, the probability of this kind of recovery is highly unlikely. Here's why.

Over the last decade, the company did not create any value for shareholders. It actually destroyed value. This creates serious doubt, going forward, that management will create value. It is not that they don't want to or that they lack the expertise, but that they cannot because of the industry in which the company operates. Competitors can produce comparable cars at lower cost, which puts pressure on GM's profits.

It is evident that companies like GM today belong to the Business C category, and investors should avoid companies with these types of economics. Intelligent investors should seek businesses from Category B.

Why are some companies able to generate high returns on capital and grow over time while others, such as GM, struggle and destroy shareholders' value? When a business can produce high returns on capital, competitors will take notice, attempt to copy it, and undercut it. Competitors force lower prices, lower market share, or both. But some businesses can resist competition and continue to earn high returns. These businesses possess some type of a competitive advantage or a moat. In his book, *The Little Book That Builds Wealth* (Wiley, 2008), Pat Dorsey explains that moats can come from the following sources:

1) Intangible Assets

2) Switching Costs

3) Network Effects

4) Cost Advantages

Intangible Assets

Types of intangible assets that create moats include brands, patents, and regulatory licenses. Some might think that the concept is simple, and as long as one buys companies with known brands, the investment will automatically be protected by a moat. However, just because a company has a known brand does not mean that the company has a moat. Everyone has heard of General Motors, but the company's performance shows no sign of a moat.

Brands that create moats allow companies to charge more for their product or to sell high volumes of products, or both. For example, Coca-Cola and Pepsi both have moats and are able sell more soft drinks than other competitors. Therefore, these companies make their money on volume, not price. An example of a brand that allows a company to charge more for its product is Ferrari. Aside from the superior quality, owning a Ferrari carries a certain amount of prestige. As a result, customers are willing to pay top dollar for it.

Patents create moats because a patent is a legal protection that stops competitors from selling the same exact product. Examples of companies with patent protections may be found in the pharmaceutical industry and the cosmetic laser industry. For example, Syneron Medical produces medical aesthetic devices that administer treatments such as hair removal, wrinkle reduction, and acne treatment. The company patented ELOS technology that combines electro and optical energy, which is safer than competing treatments. The company earned a return on equity of over 90% in 2003. In 2004, 2005, and 2006 the return on equity was over 20%.

Regulatory licenses are another form of intangible assets that allow companies to enjoy moats. Certain companies need regulatory approvals in order to operate in their industries. For example, as noted in Pat Dorsey's book, Apollo Group's University of Phoenix benefits from this type of moat because it relies on accreditation, a regulatory approval. It is very difficult to get accreditation, but once a school is approved, it is allowed to accept federal funding. Also, students may transfer credits from one accredited school to another. Schools that are accredited have an enormous advantage over ones that are not. In *Rebel with a Cause: The Entrepreneur Who Created the University of Phoenix and the For-Profit Revolution in Higher Education* (John G. Sperling, John Wiley & Sons, Inc, 2000), readers may read about the hurdles and red tape the founder of the University of Phoenix had to overcome to get approval.

Switching Costs

High switching costs present another opportunity for companies to have moats. Cell phone companies, such as Verizon Wireless, are examples of companies that benefit from switching costs. Cancellation fees, stored names and phone numbers, and the uncertainty of losing data make switching phone companies an inconvenience. Customers will avoid the inconvenience until they are sufficiently motivated to switch by poor customer service or other factors.

Another example of a company that enjoys the benefits of switching costs is Alcon. Part of its business is the development and manufacture of surgical equipment for ophthalmologists. Doctors must invest time to learn how to operate the equipment. Also, one machine may cost as much as $100,000 or more. Because of the time and money invested, they are very unlikely to switch to a competing product. In addition, Alcon's products are considered by many to be the best in the industry. In the event of litigation, surgeons may claim that they used the best equipment.

Network Effects

Network effects occur when the value of a service or product increases when more people use it. As the number of people using the product or service increases, the moat widens. For example, online dating services such as Match.com benefit from network effects. When more users post their profiles, more people want to use the site to find relationship partners because there are more people from which to choose.

Some networks are more difficult to replicate than others. The harder it is to reproduce the network, the wider the company's moat. A company can earn high returns as long as it can keep its competitors away.

Cost Advantages

Cost advantages exist when companies are able to produce a product or service more cheaply than its competitors. This is particularly valuable in commodity-type businesses where customers base purchasing decisions on price. For example, customers are indifferent about which gas station they use to purchase gas. When a company has a low cost structure, it can undercut its competitors and still make a profit. The steel industry is price sensitive, so having a low cost structure creates a moat. When steel prices decline, companies with high cost structures will start operating in the red, and companies with low cost structures will keep generating profits.

Moats Create Advantages

Companies with moats have advantages over their competitors. A good indication that a company has a moat is its earnings of high returns on equity when compared to its peers in the same industry. If a company does not earn high returns on equity, it does not have a moat, regardless of what its management says. By the same token, just because a company earns high returns on equity does not guarantee that it has a moat. Investors should investigate the reason why a company is able to earn these returns and determine if the moat is durable or if the high returns are temporary.

Sometimes it is obvious that a company has a moat, but other times it requires some research to make such a determination. For example, the management may spell out the company's competitive advantage in the annual reports. When this is not the case, investors can explore books and articles written about the industry or specific companies.

It is important to understand that moats only protect against competitors. They do not protect against demand slowdowns for products or services. For example, during the 2008-09 recession, many businesses saw their revenues decline, not because competitors gained market share but because customers worldwide cut expenditures. On a positive note, historically when demand recovered from a recession, so did revenues. But if competitors capture business, it may never return.

Obtaining Companies with Moats

Given the knowledge of what constitutes a good business, what can investors do to own one? They can either create it, or they may purchase it.

In order to create it, they can open a business like Tom did with his lemonade stand. Unfortunately, Tom's moat and returns cannot be guaranteed. The returns will depend on the type of business, competition, and capital-allocating skills. As the business grows, it will need to hire and train personnel, solicit more clients, and obtain an office or warehouse space.

Those who do not want the hassle of creating a new business may take an easier route and buy into an existing business that is already staffed and operating. In order to buy a business, investors face two more options. They can purchase it in the private market, or they can purchase it in the public market.

Private Market

The first choice for purchasing a business is buying it in the private market from an individual, a group of people, or another company. There are several disadvantages with this option.

1) Buying an entire business such as a drycleaners, a motel, or an apartment complex will require a significant amount of work unless employees are hired to operate the business.

2) Buying an entire business and then trying to sell it in the future can be difficult. A qualified buyer has to be found. The closing process is long. If money is needed quickly, liquidation may only be possible at significant discounts.

3) Unless the seller is under distress, the price is usually close to its true value. Buyers and sellers of private businesses generally have a good understanding of what their assets are worth. Approaching an owner of an apartment complex and offering to buy his or her property at 50% of its value is not likely to end with an accepted offer. This is one of the main reasons why few private companies go public during a bear market. Private owners do not want to sell their businesses to the public at discounts. During the 2008-09 bear market, many public companies were sold at prices not seen for years. For example, during the first quarter of 2009, American Express was trading at 1995 prices. The stock declined from approximately $60 to $10 – more than 80% off. Private commercial real estate was also selling at lower prices than one year earlier, but sellers were not willing or able to sell at more than 30% discounts, which is why there were fewer sales.

4) When buying an entire business, significant capital is required. There are not many private businesses that can be purchased with $1,000 of capital.

5) Because it takes so much capital to buy a private business, there are limitations on diversification. Investors might be forced to put their entire net worth into one business, and if something goes wrong, their entire investment could be eliminated.

6) Finally, transaction costs are enormous when buying and selling private businesses. A rental property worth $1,000,000 with 20% equity and 80% bank financing could cost at least $70,000 in commissions and closing costs to sell. This calculation assumes a 5% brokerage commission and a 2% closing cost (7% of $1,000,000 is $70,000). Technically, the seller is only selling his or her equity of $200,000 and is paying $70,000 to do so. Comparing equity to commissions and closing costs actually equates to a selling cost of 35% ($70,000/$200,000).

Public Market

Another way an investor can buy a business, or more specifically, part of a business, is in the public market. Buying businesses in the stock market offers some advantages over buying a business in the private market. It does not require day-to-day management, liquidation can be cheap and easy (as low as $7 to $10 per trade), it does not require significant capital, and investments can be diversified. Of all the advantages that the public market offers over private market, the most beneficial is the opportunity to buy companies below what they are actually worth. Buying $1.00 in value for $1.00 and having this dollar grow over time is good, but buying the same $1.00 in value for $0.50 is even better. This is the topic of the next chapter.

Conclusion

Good businesses are companies that generate high profits and reinvest capital at high rates. Moats protect revenues and profits from competitors, and some moats are more durable than others. Companies that can maintain an edge over their competitors are most likely to see their share prices increase over time.

Chapter 4

WHEN TO BUY

WHEN TO BUY

Deciding when to buy is just as important as deciding what to buy. Purchasing shares of a great company with a moat does not assure investment success if an investor overpays for the stock. The prices of stocks fluctuate around their values as Figure 13 below illustrates.

Fig. 13: Stock Price/Value Fluctuations

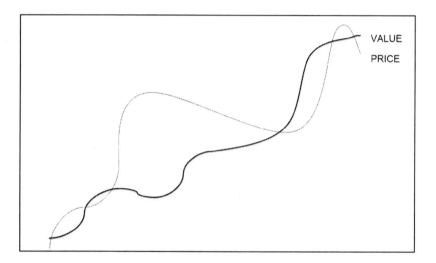

For example, in 1998, investors were willing to pay as much as $88.90 per share of Coca-Cola stock. Ten years later, it was trading as low as $40.30 and as high as $65.60. During these ten years, the company grew its earnings per share at a rate of 7.98%, had a return on shareholders' equity of over 30.00% eight years out of ten, and increased dividends at a rate of 9.74%. How is it possible that investors lost money over this ten-year period? They overpaid for the stock in 1998 by purchasing it for $88.90 per share. In 1998, the earnings per share were $1.42, which translated into a P/E ratio of 63. To justify this price, the company's earnings per share would have to grow at over 20% per year for ten years from the time the stock was purchased. It is difficult for a company of Coca-Cola's size to achieve that kind of growth, especially when from 1992 to 1998 the company had grown its earnings per share at only 12%. Because Coca-Cola grew its earnings per share at 7.98% from 1998 to 2008, it was worth approximately $30 in 1998, and the P/E ratio would have been close to 21. Investors paid almost three times what it was worth.

Another stock for which investors have overpaid is Yahoo. They were paying approximately $112 per share in 2000, but that year the company had only $0.24 in earnings per share. This was a P/E ratio of 467. To justify that price, the company would need to grow at an incredibly high rate. Because the company grew its earnings per share at 8.76% from 2000 to 2008, it actually was worth approximately $4 per share in 2000. Investors gambled on unrealistic future growth that never came.

The higher the P/E ratio, the faster the company has to grow in the future to justify the current price. Sometimes investors forget that earnings are correlated with values. They may pay prices that do not make any sense, as they did with Coca-Cola and Yahoo. When this happens, it is better to stay away from such frenzy.

But what P/E ratio is too high? To answer this question, consider the following example of a company that has earnings per share of $1. Companies usually retain a portion of earnings, but in this example the company pays out 100% of these earnings in dividends to shareholders. Would a P/E ratio of 467 for this company, as in the Yahoo example, make any sense for a potential stock purchase? This ratio would require an investor to pay $467 for the stock (467 x $1). But what does an investor get in return? He or she gets $1 per year in dividends. To pay $467 and get $1 in return equates to a return of 0.21% ($1/$467). This is less than a quarter of one percent. The bank pays eight times more. So does this make any sense? Clearly, it does not.

Would it ever make sense to pay this much? Yes, but only if the earnings grew at an extraordinary rate. If this same company with a P/E of 467 could generate earnings per share of $40 and still pay out 100% of it in dividends, the return would be 8.56% ($40/$467). Is it possible for any company to grow earnings per share from $1 to $40 in a short period of time, which equates to a total increase of 3,900%? Yes, it is possible, but is it probable? You can answer this question yourself.

What exactly is a reasonable P/E ratio to pay for a stock? One method of quickly estimating the P/E ratio is an inversion calculation. If the ratio is 10, the inversion is 1/10, which equals 10.00%. This means that if the company paid out 100% of earnings, the return on an investor's money would be 10.00%. The investor would be receiving $1.00 in earnings after paying $10.00 for the stock. If the P/E ratio is 20, the inversion is 1/20, which equals 5.00%. If the ratio is 30, the inversion is 1/30, which equals 3.33%. Therefore, investors should not pay more than a P/E ratio of 15 for companies with limited growth potential. For companies whose earnings increase at high rates, a P/E ratio of 15 to 25 may be justifiable. P/E ratios above 25 are probably too aggressive and are an indication that the stock is probably overpriced. However, there are times when a P/E ratio analysis is not all that useful. For example, when a company's earnings are temporarily depressed, the earnings variable of the ratio might be extremely small or even negative, resulting in a distorted ratio that appears large or negative.

Investment returns tend to be higher when investors buy at a discount or at least pay a fair price for companies. One of the big advantages of buying shares of companies in the public market is the ability to buy businesses for less than what they are actually worth. The practice is equivalent to buying $1.00 bills for $0.50, $0.60, or $0.70.

Figure 14 illustrates the effect of discounted purchases on returns. If an investment worth $1.00 is purchased for $1.00, and the investment value grows at 10% per year, upon the sale at the end of Year 3, the return is 33.10%. But if the same investment is purchased for $0.60, $0.50, or $0.40, the return is 123.83%, 166.20%, and 232.75% respectively.

Fig. 14: Relationship between Returns and Discounts

Price	Today	Value Year 1	Year 2	Sale Year 3	Return
$1.00	$1.00	$1.10	$1.21	$1.33	33.10%
$0.60	$1.00	$1.10	$1.21	$1.33	121.83%
$0.50	$1.00	$1.10	$1.21	$1.33	166.20%
$0.40	$1.00	$1.10	$1.21	$1.33	232.75%

Note: Dividends are not part of the calculation. Understanding discount to value is explained in more detail later in the book.

In extreme circumstances, such as the recession in 2008-09, these same $1.00 bills could be purchased for $0.10 or $0.20. Investors should be buying companies when they are trading below their values. Estimating the value of a stock is covered later in the book.

Margin of Safety

Since valuations depend on many different assumptions, a stock should only be purchased when it is trading below its value. Legendary investor Benjamin Graham refers to this approach as the *margin of safety*. In the event that an investor made a mistake and used assumptions that were never realized, he or she is somewhat protected from the full impact of his or her mistakes if the stock was purchased at a discount. Investors should always try to purchase companies for less than what they are worth. Some investment managers require a discount of 40% or more. For example, if the stock is worth $10, they will only purchase it if it is trading at $6 or less. By buying at a discount, investors protect themselves on the downside.

Why would a stock trade for less than what it is worth? In order to answer this question, one needs to understand the market on exchanges.

Trading on Exchanges

What exactly is an *exchange*? It is helpful to imagine a room where shareholders of Tom's Lemonade Enterprise visit on a daily basis to "exchange" their shares with each other. Every time they buy or sell a share, they have to pay a commission to the exchange. This is exactly what the New York Stock Exchange does, but on a much larger scale with many more companies trading hands.

On some days a stock could trade at $100, and on other days it might trade as high as $130. Upon seeing such wild price swings, everyone in the room is determined to figure out how to outsmart the others by buying at $100 and selling at $130. Because there is a tendency for people to buy when there is good news, such as the stock price increasing, there are usually people who will buy at the higher price. These price swings create opportunities for sellers to make quick profits instead of the old-fashioned way of investing and waiting for wealth accumulation over time.

To "determine" whether stock will go up or down, traders have developed a variety of theories. Some theories are based on tracking prices and trading volumes. They draw charts explaining correlations and forecasting future price directions. They use moving averages, regression analysis, and mathematical formulas. This becomes so complicated that they employ computers to help them with the task. With the "aid" of all these theories and formulas, shareholders trade their shares frequently, chasing short-term gains. Brokers and the exchange are happy with the turnover of stocks because more trading means more money to them in commissions. To increase activity, brokers and exchanges provide educational assistance to investors on how to make huge returns in the shortest time frames possible. They also provide these investors with evidence and testimonials on how other investors are able to make a lot of money trading. In other words, they do everything possible to increase the frequency of trading.

Companies are created to write computer programs that will automatically tell investors when to buy and when to sell. Advertisements typically have messages similar to the following example:

> *Start trading with our programs that will tell you exactly when to buy and when to sell. You don't have to do any research. You can trade part-time and when you make your first million, you will quit your job, enjoy your life, and live happily ever after.*

The ads offer testimonials on how the program is easy to use. They may feature a person in one of these testimonials who supposedly made $5,000 in just five minutes! Doesn't this sound wonderful?

The brokers hire analysts who follow companies and report news about them. Because Tom's Lemonade Enterprise is a public company, it is required by the SEC (Securities and Exchange Commission) to publish certain financial information for the public. Analysts study all the information carefully and interview the CEO and other key managers during quarterly conference calls. They ask for earnings guidance for the next one or two quarters. They rarely ask where the business will be in 5 to 10 years because no one is interested in such a long horizon. They compile all their information and make estimates about where the earnings will be for the next quarter or so. When the next quarter comes, depending on whether the company delivers earnings better or worse than the analysts' estimates, the stock price will soar or plummet on the news almost regardless of the long-term prospects of the company.

With all the theories, mathematical formulas, computer programs, and minute–by–minute media coverage, investing becomes so complicated that regular people who have some money to invest become thoroughly confused. They are told there is no reason to worry because help is available. Brokers, financial advisers, mutual funds, and hedge funds are happy to take investors' money and invest it for them. Because they make it seem like investing is so complicated and scary, they are able to make investors believe that everyone needs their expert advice (for which they charge a hefty fee). However, in reality, most mutual fund managers fail to generate returns better than the general market returns. Investors would be better off placing their money in a general index fund and avoid paying high management fees.

The previous paragraphs describe what the investment world has become over many years. Investors with a long-term horizon can exploit this type of short-term mentality. The 2008-09 recession and the events that affected AIG, Lehman Brothers and other companies made many stocks trade at unusually low prices. It is tragic that so many people lost a significant amount of money in the market as a result of these events. However, the future can be bright for investors if they position their investment dollars in the right companies when this kind of opportunity arises. When economies recover, good companies survive and their stock prices recover.

How to Take Advantage of a Shortsighted Market

Have you ever thought of the short-term market as being like a voting machine? What about the long-term market as a weighing machine? Benjamin Graham coined the well-known "voting machine" analogy and went on to describe the long-term market as a "weighing machine." (*The Intelligent Investor: The definitive book on value investing. A book of practical counsel.* Revised ed. Collins Business. 2003.) What did this famous advocate of "loss minimization" mean by these phrases?

The "voting" aspect of the stock market is a popularity contest where participants try to determine which stocks will have gains over the next 3 to 12 months. The "weighing" aspect of the stock market means that over the long run, fundamentals will be weighed correctly, and the prices ultimately will reflect the underlying values.

The majority of the investment community, including money managers and individual investors, are short-term motivated. Hedge fund managers are heavily influenced by quarterly and yearly performances. Some of them report progress to their clients weekly. If the quarterly or yearly performance is negative, clients take their money elsewhere, and the money managers are out of jobs unless they can convince other managers' clients that they are the "elsewhere" to park their investments.

Because of these pressures, investment managers are unlikely to buy shares of companies that are not going to appreciate within 12 months. Even if they find investment opportunities that can be bought at 70% discounts, they will not buy them unless these investments are likely to appreciate within a few quarters. The same principle applies to investments that are likely to decline in price within a year. Investment managers will sell simply because the price might decline in the short term. The company could be excellent and have a superb long-term outlook, but unless the short-term price movement is positive, these shortsighted managers will sell the stock.

This sounds absurd, and perhaps it is, but the reality is that it happens all the time. Investors who understand the short-term motivation and pressures that most money managers face can profit handsomely by buying great businesses at favorable prices irrespective of their short-term outlook.

Events that create opportunities for long-term investors are *bear markets, industry-specific recessions,* and *the unpopularity of individual companies.* These events create uncertainties that the short-term investment community does not handle well.

> **To make the most of shortsighted behavior, investors should seek investment opportunities with short-term uncertainty and long-term certainty.**

Bear Markets

Bear markets occur when the stock market steadily falls for a prolonged period of time. They are great buying opportunities because of the fear factor. As stock prices decline, more investors sell, fearing further declines. Individuals watching their investments decline in value contact their money managers and ask for their money back with *redemption requests*. These managers have to sell investments to satisfy redemptions, forcing prices to collapse even further. The media exacerbates the vicious cycle by continually reminding the investment community of the declines, creating even more fear. As there are more sellers than buyers, prices become so depressed that companies start trading at prices significantly below their values. This is exactly what happened worldwide from 2007 to 2009.

Industry-Specific Recessions

At times, specific industries might experience recessions. Individual companies within these industries may be sold by institutions and individual investors because of uncertain outlooks. An investor's job is to assess whether the industry recession is short-term or long-term in nature. The investor may ask himself or herself if the specific industry is experiencing a slowdown because technology is replacing its products or for a different reason. For example, companies in the video and DVD rental business have been experiencing negative consequences because of new technology and the Internet. It is unlikely that this trend will abate because the Internet and technology are changing this particular industry permanently. Companies in the airline industry faced tough times after the September 11, 2001 attack, but after some time had lapsed, travelers returned to flying.

Unpopularity of Individual Companies

Prices of individual companies may become depressed for many reasons such as missing quarterly estimates, negative publicity, or a bleak short-term outlook. If the moat and the long-term outlook of an individual company did not change because of these events, depressed prices should be viewed as buying opportunities.

Conclusion

Knowing that most of the investment community is oriented toward the short term, buying shares of excellent companies for less than they are worth is a smart way to invest. Finding out the price is easy because it is quoted by exchanges. Determining the value is a bit more complicated. This is the focus of the next chapter.

Chapter 5

How To Value
A Company

HOW TO VALUE A COMPANY

What is *value*? Merriam-Webster's Online Dictionary has several definitions, including the "relative <u>worth</u>, utility, or importance" or "the monetary <u>worth</u> of something." OK, so what is *worth*? Again, Merriam-Webster says *worth* is "the <u>value</u> of something measured by its qualities or by the esteem in which it is held." (http://www.merriam-webster.com)

Given these circular definitions, is it fair to say that it all depends on who is asked? Some will say that *value* is the price that the highest bidder is willing to pay for something. For example, some would say that an apartment building is worth $1,000,000 because several buyers are offering to buy it for that price. However, a better definition of value is described by Warren Buffett who says that value is what a buyer receives when making a purchase. In other words, price is what one must pay in order to receive something of value. The relative price of stocks in a moment in time is easy to determine with certainty: prices are quoted by exchanges constantly and made available on the Internet in near real time. Value, on the other hand, is much more difficult to determine.

Once the value is estimated, it is possible to determine if a stock is trading at a discount or at a premium to its value. In other words, it can be determined if purchasing a particular stock for a particular price is a good deal.

What are investors really buying when purchasing shares?

Because investors become owners of companies when they purchase company shares, they need to think like owners. Owners of rental properties receive the benefit of rental income from tenants. When the rental income exceeds expenses such as real estate taxes, insurance, maintenance, and interest on the loan, the owner may pocket positive cash flow that is generated. The same applies to being a shareholder of any company. A company generates revenues and incurs expenses. Net income is positive if revenues exceed expenses. Although the net income actually belongs to the shareholders, only a certain portion, if any, is paid in the form of dividends. The rest is reinvested. Companies that grow aggressively may reinvest all of their earnings and not pay any dividends in order to maximize growth.

To illustrate this point, let us imagine that a fictitious company has earnings per share of $2.00 and that 30% of the earnings are paid out in the form of dividends. Dividends are $0.60 per share ($2.00 x 30%). The rest is retained and reinvested for the shareholders. From the investors' perspective, dividends are the income stream because they are what investors receive in cash. Because a portion of earnings is retained by the company and reinvested to produce still greater earnings, dividends are expected to grow as the earnings grow. The current and estimated future dividend income streams are part of what gives perceived value to a company. Estimating the future income streams makes it possible to estimate *current value*.

So what is a company worth? Before answering this question, some understanding of basic financial theory is required.

Basic Finance

To begin the discussion of how we can use dividend projections to estimate the *current value* of a stock, let us use the simple example of money in a bank account. If we deposit $10 in the bank today, what will it be worth three years from now if the bank pays 2% in interest per year?

A good way to think about this is to imagine a very slow elevator that takes one year to travel from floor to floor. Our $10 deposit begins in the lobby. At each floor, the money in the elevator grows by the interest rate. This is illustrated in Figure 15.

Fig. 15: Growth over 3 years at a 2% interest rate

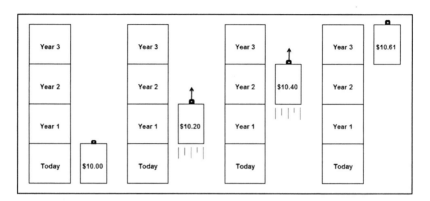

The $10.00 leaves the lobby and as it reaches Level 1 after one year, it has grown by 2% to $10.20. In order to calculate this, we multiply $10.00 by 1 plus 2% or 1.02. This gives us $10.00 x 1.02 = $10.20.

By the time it arrives at Level 3 or Year 3, the account is now worth $10.61. So, $10 in the bank today receiving a 2% return will be worth $10.61 in three years ($10.00 x 1.02 x 1.02 x 1.02 = $10.61).

Although a 2% interest from a bank account appeared attractive when many other types of investments were losing money in 2008, we have grown accustomed to getting a better return and seek out a better return for our investments. So, what will $10 in the bank today be worth in three years if the bank pays 5% per year instead of 2%? Figure 16 shows us that it will be worth $11.58 ($10.00 x 1.05 x 1.05 x 1.05 = $11.58).

Fig. 16: Growth over 3 years at 5% interest rate

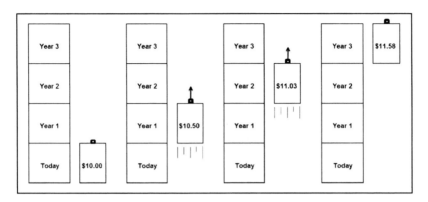

The two previous illustrations are examples of *compounding*. A pretty smart fellow, Albert Einstein, once said that compound interest was the most powerful force in the universe. Compounding is the process of adding interest to the original principal and allowing the new principal sum to earn interest that can be added to the accumulating principal, and so on. Both Figures 15 and 16 illustrate compounding; note that while the interest rate went up 2.5 times from 2% to 5%, the dollar amount difference went up 2.59 times.

What about working backwards from a financial goal? Let's say that we want to have a sum of $12 in three years. How much money would we need to put in the bank today to have $12 in three years, assuming the bank will pay 3% interest? These calculations are more difficult than our previous ones, but they lie at the heart of methods called *discounting* that are used to value companies and their stocks. There are numerous models and methods such as the Gordon Model, the average growth approximation method, and the discounted cash flow (DCF) method that are used to estimate the potential market prices of stocks.

In our elevator illustration, the elevator's descent represents discounting. When it begins its descent, it contains the target sum of $12, which is our original goal three years out.

Fig. 17: Amount needed in the bank today to have $12 in 3 years

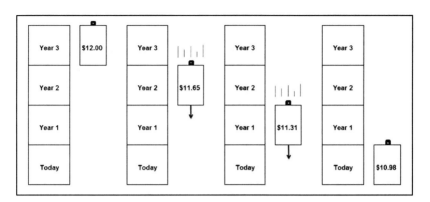

When the elevator rose one level at a time, the money increased yearly by a compounding of the interest rate. When the elevator descends each level, the money is decreased by the interest rate. As $12.00 travels down one level, it decreases to $11.65. This calculation is achieved by taking $12.00 divided (not multiplied) by 1 plus 0.03 (the 3% interest rate). This is $12.00/1.03 = $11.65.

We do this calculation every time the elevator passes each level. So, $12.00 is decreased to $11.65 in Year 2. Then $11.65 is decreased to $11.31 in Year 1. Finally $11.31 is decreased to $10.98 today.

Our calculations in Figure 17 show that in order to have $12.00 in three years, an investment of $10.98 is needed in the bank today, assuming the bank pays 3% on the money.

What if the bank pays more than 3%? Figure 18 illustrates this important concept: the more the bank pays, the less we have to place in the bank to end up with $12.00 in three years.

Fig. 18: Effects of varying discount rates

	Discount Rate 3%	Results	Discount Rate 5%	Results	Discount Rate 10%	Results
End of Year 3		$12.00		$12.00		$12.00
End of Year 2	$12.00/1.03	$11.65	$12.00/1.05	$11.43	$12.00/1.1	$10.91
End of Year 1	$11.65/1.03	$11.31	$11.43/1.05	$10.88	$10.91/1.1	$9.92
Today	$11.31/1.03	$10.98	$10.88/1.05	$10.37	$9.92/1.1	$9.02

Figure 18 shows that we would only need to invest $10.37 instead of $10.98 to have $12.00 in three years if the bank paid 5% instead of 3%. If the bank paid 10%, the initial investment required decreases to $9.02.

In other words,

- $10.98 is equal to $12.00 in three years if the interest rate is 3%,

- $10.37 is equal to $12.00 in three years if the interest rate is 5%, and

- $9.02 is equal to $12.00 in three years if the interest rate is 10%.

They are equal because an investor would be indifferent if he or she had

- $10.98 today or $12.00 in three years, assuming 3% interest rate;

- $10.37 today or $12.00 in three years, assuming 5% interest rate; or

- $9.02 today or $12.00 in three years, assuming 10% interest rate.

All of the above is just a complicated way of saying

- $12.00 in three years is worth $10.98 today, assuming 3% interest rate;

- $12.00 in three years is worth $10.37 today, assuming 5% interest rate; and

- $12.00 in three years is worth $9.02 today, assuming 10% interest rate.

It is important to observe that the only changing variable is the interest rate. As the interest rate increases, today's value becomes smaller. This happens because we are discounting the $12.00 at a higher interest rate. The interest rate that we use to discount values to the present is called a *discount rate*. In the previous illustrations, the discount rate is 3%, 5%, or 10%. If the discount rate is 3%, then $12.00 in three years is worth $10.98 today. If the discount rate is 5%, then $12.00 in three years is worth $10.37 today. If the discount rate is 10%, then $12.00 in three years is worth $9.02 today.

By knowing how to calculate the value of future money, we are able to determine the value of a company once we estimate the future income that as owners/investors we will receive. But because the value depends on the discount rate used, how do we know which rate to use? It depends on the riskiness or certainty of the expected future income. A discount rate is nothing more than an investor's required rate of return. If an investment carries more risk or uncertainty, an investor is going to require a higher discount rate (required rate of return) to compensate for the higher risk being assumed. This is similar to a bank requiring a higher interest rate on a loan to a borrower with a weaker credit score. The bank expects to be compensated for the additional risk.

Choosing the Appropriate Discount Rate

The level of an investor's required rate of return (the discount rate) on an investment affects today's perceived value of an investment. The higher the discount rate, the lower today's perceived value will be. So, how high or low should the discount rate be set? Different investors use different methods of estimating an appropriate discount rate. Some use mathematical formulas and others just choose a number.

The best approach is to keep it simple and use common sense. If a bank pays 2.0% for deposits, it would not make any sense for the discount rate to be below this number. Stock returns are far more uncertain than returns from the bank. Investors need to require a higher return to compensate for the uncertainty. In this example, we know the discount rate has to be greater than 2.0%.

The U.S. government issues treasury bonds to finance its operations. The rates that the government will pay vary from time to time, depending on the overall economy and other factors. Because the government can raise taxes and print money, investments in government securities are considered risk-free, meaning that the government will not default. Therefore, if the government is paying from 3% to 4%, the discount rate for stocks needs to be higher than that to compensate for the uncertainty that stocks carry.

Just as the government does, various types of companies issue corporate bonds to finance their operations. Bondholders receive their interest payments before shareholders ever receive a single dollar in dividends. So, the bondholders' position is less risky than the position of shareholders. If the corporate bonds pay from 5% to 7%, the discount rate for stocks must be higher than that.

The rate that different institutions pay to borrow money, whether they are banks, governments, or corporations, depends on the probability of repayment. The discount rate used to calculate values of stocks needs to be higher than the rates that these institutions pay for bonds because returns on stocks are more uncertain. But some corporations' returns on stocks are more predictable than others. For example, returns from Coca-Cola are much more predictable than those from some high-tech company that may be bankrupt within a year or two. The discount rate for Coca-Cola would be lower than the discount rate of a more unpredictable company.

It is relatively safe to say that an appropriate discount rate for stock valuations should be between 7% and 13%. Very predictable companies could have discount rates in the lower range, and less predictable companies should have discount rates in the upper range. In our calculations, we use a 10% discount rate.

Valuing a Stock

An investment may pay *dividends* for many years. For example, it could pay dividends in the following way:

$12.05 in Year 1

$12.14 in Year 2

$13.50 in Year 3

The determination of the value of all of these dividends is similar to asking three separate questions:

What is $12.05 in one year worth today?

What is $12.14 in two years worth today?

What is $13.50 in three years worth today?

Answering each question and adding up the answers would equate to the current value of the income stream of these dividends spread across three years. The value of the dividend income stream can again be illustrated using the elevator analogy to answer the first question:

What is $12.05 in one year worth today?

In Figure 19, the elevator starts at Year 1 with the $12.05 dividend. Again, we take $12.05 and divide it by 1 plus 10%, which is our discount rate. One plus 10% is the same as 1.10. Therefore, a dividend of $12.05 that is to be realized a year from now is worth $10.95 ($12.05/1.1) today.

Fig. 19: Bringing $12.05 to the Lobby or Today

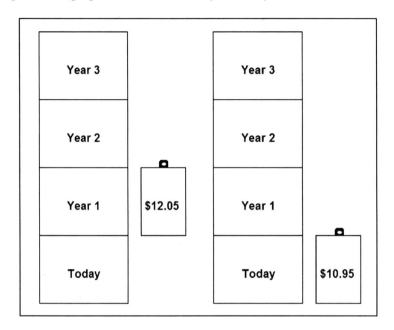

What is $12.14 in two years worth today?

In Figure 20, the elevator starts at Year 2 with a dividend of $12.14. This dividend is worth $11.04 ($12.14/1.1) in Year 1 and $10.03 ($11.04/1.1) today. A shortcut calculation could be used as follows:

$$\frac{\$12.14}{(1.1 \times 1.1)}$$

Fig. 20: Bringing $12.14 to the Lobby or Today

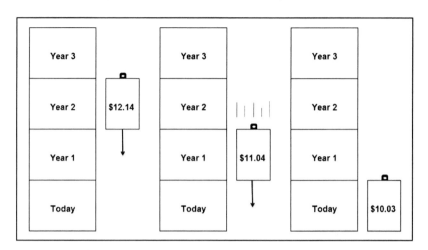

What is $13.50 in three years worth today?

In Figure 21, the elevator starts on level 3, picks up $13.50 in dividends and brings it to the lobby. In Year 2, it is worth $12.27 ($13.50/1.1). In Year 1, it is worth $11.16 ($12.27/1.1). Finally, it is worth $10.14 ($11.16/1.1) today. A shortcut calculation could be used as follows:

$$\frac{\$13.50}{(1.1 \times 1.1 \times 1.1)}$$

Fig. 21: Bringing $13.50 to the Lobby or Today

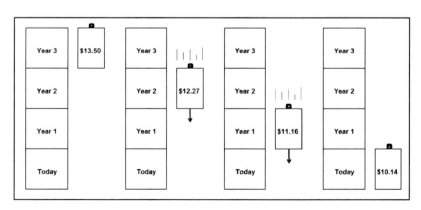

The current value of each of the three future dividends is calculated separately, and then added together to determine the current value of the income stream.

Question: What is a dividend of $12.05 in one year worth today? *Answer:* $10.95

Question: What is a dividend of $12.14 in two years worth today? *Answer:* $10.03

Question: What is a dividend of $13.50 in three years worth today? *Answer:* $10.14

Using a discount rate of 10%, the current discounted value of the dividend income stream over a three-year period is $31.12.

$12.05 in Year 1	$10.95
$12.14 in Year 2	$10.03
$13.50 in Year 3	$10.14
	$31.12

Dividends are only one source of an income stream or cash flow from an investment. If only dividends counted, companies that paid no dividends would be worthless. What else does an investor get when owning a stock? An investor also gets the sale proceeds when he or she sells a stock in the future. The projected sale price has to be taken into account in the value calculation even if the investor does not sell it. We assume that the investor sells it because he or she could sell it if desired. Assuming that an investor could sell the stock in our previous example for $200 at the end of Year 3, what would this stock sale price be worth today? It definitely would not be worth $200 because the money from the sale would not be received until three years from now. Just as all the dividends were discounted, this lump sum of money from the stock sale also has to be discounted. See the illustration in Figure 22.

Fig. 22: Bringing $200 to the Lobby or Today

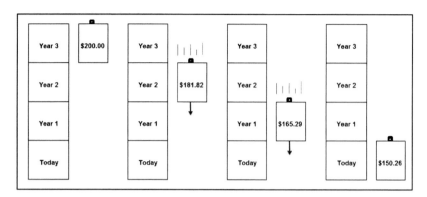

Figure 22 illustrates how $200 from the sale of the stock is discounted to the present by using a discount rate of 10%. The calculation of the discounted value is $200/(1.1 x 1.1 x 1.1) equals $150.26. So, the sale of stock at $200 three years from now is valued at $150.26 today.

Considering the income stream and the stock sale at the end of the three-year holding period, what is today's total value of the stock? Remember that the discounted value of the dividend income stream is $31.12 and the discounted value of the sale price is $150.26. The total value of the stock is the sum of both: $31.12 plus $150.26 equals $181.38.

Valuing Companies Using a Spreadsheet

The elevator analogy in the previous paragraphs was used to illustrate how discounting works. Calculating values by hand is time-consuming. Thanks to spreadsheet software such as Microsoft Excel, these value calculations can be done in seconds, as demonstrated on the following page. The spreadsheet template that we are using in Figure 23 for the discussion that follows may be downloaded at www.ClassicValueInvestors.com.

Fig. 23: Spreadsheet Valuation Template

FACTS	VARIABLES	VALUE CALCULATIONS			
Current Trading Price	$55.00		Projected	Payout	Dividends	Discounted
Current Earnings Per Share	$5.50	Year	Earnings	Ratio		Dividends
Current P/E Ratio	10.0	1	$6.16	30%	$1.85	$1.68
Dividend Payout	30%	2	$6.90	30%	$2.07	$1.71
		3	$7.73	30%	$2.32	$1.74
ASSUMPTIONS		4	$8.65	30%	$2.60	$1.77
Earnings Growth Rate (1st Five Years)	12.00%	5	$9.69	30%	$2.91	$1.81
Earnings Growth Rate (2nd Five Years)	9.00%	6	$10.57	30%	$3.17	$1.79
Discount Rate	10.0%	7	$11.52	30%	$3.45	$1.77
P/E Ratio in 10 Years	15	8	$12.55	30%	$3.77	$1.76
		9	$13.68	30%	$4.10	$1.74
RESULTS		10	$14.91	30%	$4.47	$1.72
Value of Future Dividends Today	$17.50					$17.50
Value of Future Sales Price Today	$86.25					
Value of the Stock	$103.74	10	Projected	P/E Ratio in	Terminal	Discounted
			Earnings	10 Years	Value	Terminal Value
			$14.91	15	$223.71	$86.25
Discount to Value	46.98%					

Investors enter variable information in the cells that are shaded gray and bolded. The only factual information that investors need to enter is the current trading price, earnings per share, and dividend payout. Dividend payout is the percentage of earnings that is paid out in dividends. This information is readily available in company financial statements.

Now back to Figure 23. Investors need to enter data into the spreadsheet for assumptions about the future such as the growth rate for the first five and second five years, the investor's discount rate, and the estimated P/E ratio in 10 years. Ten years is the holding period used in this particular valuation. In Figure 23, the growth rate used for the first five years is 12% and for the second five years is 9%. We set the discount rate at 10%, and we will assume that the P/E ratio in 10 years will be 15.

Once the information is entered, the valuation model will show the growth of projected earnings for ten years on the right side of the chart. In our example, projected earnings will be $6.16 in Year 1 and $14.91 in Year 10. The payout ratio will be used to determine dividends. Since we assumed the payout ratio is 30% in our example, dividends in Year 1 are projected to be $1.85 ($6.16 x 30%) and in Year 10 are projected to be $4.47 ($14.91 x 30%). Today, these future dividends are not worth the same as shown in the dividends column. Because they will be received in the future, they have to be discounted to determine their current value. The column called *Discounted Dividends* shows the results of those calculations. For example, the $1.85 dividend projected in Year 1 is worth $1.68 today. The $3.77 dividend projected in Year 8 is only worth $1.76 today. Every single projected future dividend has some value today. When the 10 years of discounted projected dividends are added together, today's value of all the dividends totals to $17.50.

But as mentioned before, dividends are only one source of income. The second source is the sale price at the end of the holding period. This price is called the *terminal value*. We know that the earnings per share are projected in Year 10 to be $14.91, and the assumed P/E ratio in ten years is projected to be 15. The formula for the terminal value is the earnings per share times the P/E ratio. Based on the assumptions we used for this example, the *Terminal Value* or sales price in ten years is $223.71. But again, the value today of a projected future value of $223.71 is not actually $223.71 because this amount will not be received for 10 years. The discounted value today of this future projected lump sum is $86.25, which is shown under the *Discounted Terminal Value* heading in the bottom right of corner in Figure 23.

Under the **RESULTS** heading in Figure 23, today's value of projected future dividends, $17.50, is added with today's value of the future sales price, $86.25, to arrive at today's value of the stock, which in this case is $103.74. The model also calculates a *Discount to Value*. Note that *discount to value* is different from the *discount rate*. In this case, today's value of the stock is $103.74, and today's trading price is $55.00. In other words, by paying $55.00 for something that is worth $103.74 today, it is equivalent to getting a 46.98% *discount to value* or buying $1.00 in value for $0.53.

Estimating the value of a company depends on assumptions such as the growth rate, discount rate, dividend payout, and terminal value. Investors should use conservative assumptions. For example, if a company grew its earnings at 10% over the past ten years, it is unrealistic to think that they can grow them at 17% over the next ten years. Such growth is possible, but there should be a good reason for making the assumption that it will grow at a higher rate.

In the analysis, investors should try different scenarios when valuing a stock. They should ask the following questions:

What is the estimated value of the stock if <u>conservative</u> assumptions are used?

What is the estimated value of the stock if <u>more conservative</u> assumptions are used?

What is the estimated value of the stock if <u>more aggressive</u> assumptions are used?

To illustrate, let's try the model using the same facts as before, but changing the assumptions.

Scenario #1: Conservative Assumptions

Question: What is the estimated value of the company if its earnings per share grow at 12% for the first five years and 9% for the second five years, the terminal P/E ratio is 15, and the discount rate is 10%?

Fig. 24: Conservative Model

FACTS	VARIABLES			VALUE CALCULATIONS			
Current Trading Price	$55.00			Projected	Payout	Dividends	Discounted
Current Earnings Per Share	$5.50	Year	Earnings	Ratio			Dividends
Current P/E Ratio	10.0	1	$6.16	30%	$1.85		$1.68
Dividend Payout	30%	2	$6.90	30%	$2.07		$1.71
		3	$7.73	30%	$2.32		$1.74
ASSUMPTIONS		4	$8.65	30%	$2.60		$1.77
Earnings Growth Rate (1st Five Years)	12.00%	5	$9.69	30%	$2.91		$1.81
Earnings Growth Rate (2nd Five Years)	9.00%	6	$10.57	30%	$3.17		$1.79
Discount Rate	10.0%	7	$11.52	30%	$3.45		$1.77
P/E Ratio in 10 Years	15	8	$12.55	30%	$3.77		$1.76
		9	$13.68	30%	$4.10		$1.74
RESULTS		10	$14.91	30%	$4.47		$1.72
Value of Future Dividends Today	$17.50						$17.50
Value of Future Sales Price Today	$86.25						
Value of the Stock	$103.74	10	Projected	P/E Ratio in	Terminal	Discounted
			Earnings	10 Years	Value	Terminal Value
			$14.91	15	$223.71	$86.25
Discount to Value	46.98%						

Note that these are the same assumptions used in the calculation scenario shown in Figure 23. Based on these previously used assumptions, the estimated value of the stock is $103.74. Purchasing it for $55.00 would mean getting a 46.98% discount or buying $1.00 in value for $0.53.

Scenario #2: More Conservative Assumptions

Question: What is the estimated value of the same company if its earnings per share grow at 9% for the first five years and 7% for the second five years, the terminal P/E ratio is 10, and the discount rate is 10%?

Fig. 25: More Conservative Model

FACTS	VARIABLES		VALUE CALCULATIONS			
Current Trading Price	$55.00		Projected	Payout	Dividends	Discounted
Current Earnings Per Share	$5.50	Year	Earnings	Ratio		Dividends
Current P/E Ratio	10.0	1	$6.00	30%	$1.80	$1.64
Dividend Payout	30%	2	$6.53	30%	$1.96	$1.62
		3	$7.12	30%	$2.14	$1.61
ASSUMPTIONS		4	$7.76	30%	$2.33	$1.59
Earnings Growth Rate (1st Five Years)	9.00%	5	$8.46	30%	$2.54	$1.58
Earnings Growth Rate (2nd Five Years)	7.00%	6	$9.05	30%	$2.72	$1.53
Discount Rate	10.0%	7	$9.69	30%	$2.91	$1.49
P/E Ratio in 10 Years	10	8	$10.37	30%	$3.11	$1.45
		9	$11.09	30%	$3.33	$1.41
RESULTS		10	$11.87	30%	$3.56	$1.37
Value of Future Dividends Today	$15.29					$15.29
Value of Future Sales Price Today	$45.76					
Value of the Stock	$61.05	10	Projected	P/E Ratio in	Terminal	Discounted
			Earnings	10 Years	Value	Terminal Value
			$11.87	10	$118.69	$45.76
Discount to Value	9.91%					

Based on the more conservative assumptions, the estimated value of the stock is $61.05. Purchasing it for $55.00 would mean getting a 9.91% discount or buying $1.00 in value for $0.90.

Scenario #3: More Aggressive Assumptions

Question: What is the estimated value of the company if its earnings per share grow at 15% for the next ten years, the terminal P/E ratio is 15, and the discount rate is 10%?

Fig. 26: More Aggressive Model

FACTS	VARIABLES		VALUE CALCULATIONS			
Current Trading Price	$55.00		Projected	Payout	Dividends	Discounted
Current Earnings Per Share	$5.50	Year	Earnings	Ratio		Dividends
Current P/E Ratio	10.0	1	$6.33	30%	$1.90	$1.73
Dividend Payout	30%	2	$7.27	30%	$2.18	$1.80
		3	$8.36	30%	$2.51	$1.89
ASSUMPTIONS		4	$9.62	30%	$2.89	$1.97
Earnings Growth Rate (1st Five Years)	15.00%	5	$11.06	30%	$3.32	$2.06
Earnings Growth Rate (2nd Five Years)	15.00%	6	$12.72	30%	$3.82	$2.15
Discount Rate	10.0%	7	$14.63	30%	$4.39	$2.25
P/E Ratio in 10 Years	15	8	$16.82	30%	$5.05	$2.35
		9	$19.35	30%	$5.80	$2.46
RESULTS		10	$22.25	30%	$6.68	$2.57
Value of Future Dividends Today	$21.24					$21.24
Value of Future Sales Price Today	$128.68					
Value of the Stock	$149.92	10	Projected	P/E Ratio in	Terminal	Discounted
			Earnings	10 Years	Value	Terminal Value
			$22.25	15	$333.76	$128.68
Discount to Value	63.31%					

Based on more aggressive assumptions, the value of the stock is $149.92. Purchasing it for $55.00 would mean getting a 63.31% discount or buying $1.00 in value for $0.37.

Reconciliation of Value

Using different scenarios, it can be seen that the estimated value of a company depends on certain assumptions about the future. Nobody knows exactly what the future holds. So, how can anyone determine the value of a stock with any precision? We don't think anyone can. The good news is that it is not important to know exactly what something is worth to get an idea of whether or not it is trading at a discount. In our three-scenario analysis, the stock is currently worth anywhere between $61 and $150, which is a huge range. If the stock is trading at $130, it is not hard to realize that there is not much discount being offered. But what happens if the stock is trading at $30? In this case it does not really matter whether the stock is worth $61 or $150. In either case, it is a screaming deal!

Increasing the Probabilities of Being Right

Because the value depends so much on estimates and assumptions, is there a possibility of increasing the accuracy of these guesses? Yes, there is. The best way to achieve more predictable results is to invest in simple and predictable businesses.

Companies in rapidly changing industries are unpredictable and difficult to value. For example, looking at the last 10 years of earnings for the following two companies, it is evident that Company A has a more predictable pattern of earnings than Company B.

Fig. 27: Earnings Patterns

EPS	Company A	Company B
Year 1	$1.02	$1.02
Year 2	$1.12	$0.50
Year 3	$1.25	$2.30
Year 4	$1.36	-$0.30
Year 5	$1.34	$0.40
Year 6	$1.51	$0.60
Year 7	$1.58	$0.02
Year 8	$1.74	$1.50
Year 9	$2.26	$1.75
Year 10	$2.31	$0.85

By looking at Company A's earnings pattern, investors can make reasonable assumptions about the future. Earnings of Company B are unpredictable and no assumptions can be made except that earnings are likely to continue to be unpredictable. Company A's past earnings pattern provides investors with better long-term certainty.

When predicting future earnings, investors should try to imagine what the company will look like in 10 to 20 years. For example, Coca-Cola will probably still be selling soft drinks 10 years from now. Budweiser will probably still be selling beer 10 years from now. The Internet or technology might change how soft drinks or beer are marketed or manufactured, but they will not significantly change how these products are consumed.

What about companies such as Yahoo and Google? Will they still be around in 10 to 20 years? This is more difficult to answer because their businesses are based on technology that changes constantly. At one time, Yahoo was the top search engine. Then, Google surpassed it. Google is now not only the most popular search engine, but also the company is changing the world of advertising. Will there be another company to replace Google in the future? Maybe, or maybe not—the long-term future is uncertain. Technology can create fortunes for companies, but it can also destroy them seemingly overnight.

Investing in businesses that are predictable in the long run makes them easier to value. Predicting the unpredictable is better left for the rocket scientists on Wall Street.

Understanding Discount to Value and Return

In our previous analysis, the *discount to value* ranged between 9.91% and 63.31%, depending on the assumptions we made. It is easy to conceptualize that getting a bigger discount is better than getting a smaller discount. As mentioned previously, the higher the discount, the higher the return. Here is the explanation of why this is true.

The three scenarios of valuation presented had different effects on our returns. For example, Scenario #1 gave us an estimated value of $103.74 based on a conservative set of variables. If the future assumptions prove true in the exact fashion as projected under Scenario #1, and we pay exactly $103.74 for the stock, which is equal to its value, our return on the money will be 10% per year for the next 10 years. It will be equal to the discount rate that we required in the first place. If we refuse to pay the price equal to the value and buy the stock at a discount, our return will be higher than 10%. The higher the discount, the higher the return will be. If we choose to pay more for the stock than it is worth, our return will be less than 10%.

What will our return be if all the assumptions in Scenario #1 happen exactly as predicted, and we pay $55 for the stock when it is worth $103.74? We already know that the return will be more than 10% because we are buying the stock at a discount. To be more exact, we can use the valuation model again and manipulate the discount rate until the value of the stock equals its price. See Figure 28.

Fig. 28: Value Equals Trading Price

FACTS	VARIABLES	VALUE CALCULATIONS			
Current Trading Price	$55.00		Projected	Payout	Dividends	Discounted
Current Earnings Per Share	$5.50	Year	Earnings	Ratio		Dividends
Current P/E Ratio	10.0	1	$6.16	30%	$1.85	$1.57
Dividend Payout	30%	2	$6.90	30%	$2.07	$1.49
		3	$7.73	30%	$2.32	$1.41
ASSUMPTIONS		4	$8.65	30%	$2.60	$1.34
Earnings Growth Rate (1st Five Years)	12.00%	5	$9.69	30%	$2.91	$1.27
Earnings Growth Rate (2nd Five Years)	9.00%	6	$10.57	30%	$3.17	$1.18
Discount Rate	17.96%	7	$11.52	30%	$3.45	$1.09
P/E Ratio in 10 Years	15	8	$12.55	30%	$3.77	$1.00
		9	$13.68	30%	$4.10	$0.93
RESULTS		10	$14.91	30%	$4.47	$0.86
Value of Future Dividends Today	$12.13					$12.13
Value of Future Sales Price Today	$42.89					
Value of the Stock	$55.02	10	Projected Earnings	P/E Ratio in 10 Years	Terminal Value	Discounted Terminal Value
			$14.91	15	$223.71	$42.89
Discount to Value	0.04%					

In Figure 28, the assumptions about the future are exactly the same as the assumptions from Scenario #1. The only difference is the discount rate. By trial and error, the discount rate is increased until the value of the stock is as close as possible to the trading price. This result is achieved in this example when the discount rate is 17.96%. Note that in this case, the discount to value is almost 0%. (It is 0.04%, to be precise.) What this tells us is that if the future happens as estimated, and we pay $55 for the stock, we can expect to earn 17.96% on our money every year for the next 10 years.

Choosing the P/E Ratio in 10 Years

The estimated price at which the stock will sell at the end of the holding period will affect the value of the stock today. Usually companies with moats trade at higher P/E ratios compared to companies without moats, just like better cars, such as BMWs, sell for more money than Fords. A good way to describe a P/E ratio is the price to pay for a dollar of earnings. For example if the earnings are $1.00 and the P/E ratio is 15, then the price for this $1.00 of earnings is 15. Companies that possess moats are better than companies without moats, and therefore, require a higher price as reflected by a higher P/E ratio.

Because we live in a capitalistic world, competitors are continuously attacking the moats of companies that possess them. As mentioned before, some moats are more durable and harder to overcome than others. Just as invaders of castles were eventually able to cross the moats, competitors are likely to overcome moats that protect companies. Because of this, it is advisable to assume that the moat will be weaker or completely gone at the end of the holding period, and therefore, its price will be lower in relation to its earnings and will trade at a lower P/E ratio. Using an estimated P/E ratio between 12 and 15 at the end of the holding period is likely to be a safe bet. A P/E ratio of more than 15 or 20 is probably too aggressive. If the company does retain its moat and trade at high P/E ratios at the end of the holding period, this is a bonus, but it is always safer to use conservative assumptions for the P/E ratio in the valuation model.

Conclusion

The value of a company is an important factor to consider in determining if buying its stock is a good deal. Valuations depend on factors such as discount rates, growth rates, and terminal values. Many investors and analysts estimate and express the value in terms of a single number. However, it is almost impossible to be exact because there are too many moving parts.

Investors should change various variables in the calculations and estimate different values and ranges, then compare them to the trading prices. Stocks should only be purchased when the price is favorable compared to the value. Being exact is not that important. Whether a stock is worth $20, $15, or $30 should not change a buying decision for a stock that is trading for $5. BUY IT!

Chapter 6

BASIC CAPITAL STRUCTURE

BASIC CAPITAL STRUCTURE

Every business, whether it is a transportation company or an Internet company, has assets that generate revenues. These assets have to be financed either by equity, liabilities (debt is a type of liability), or a combination thereof. The company in the following illustration has $100 in assets. Because there is no debt, the equity portion is also $100. In this case, Assets = Equity.

Fig. 29: Assets financed with 100% Equity

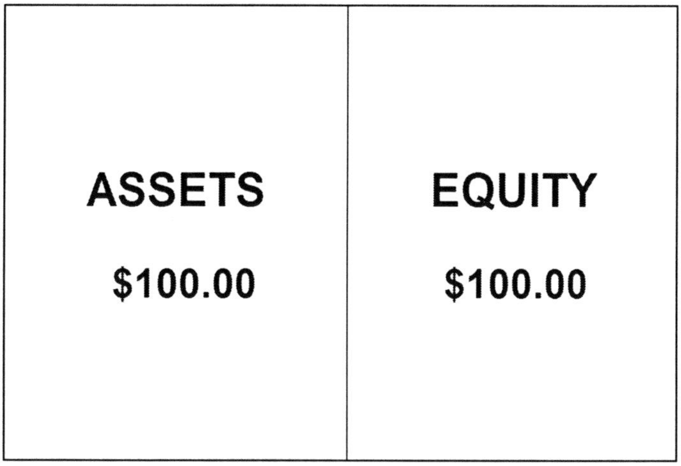

ASSETS	EQUITY
$100.00	$100.00

If the company generates $10 in earnings for the year, the return on equity is 10% ($10/$100). This ratio is important because it indicates how profitable a company is in relation to the original equity investment. The right side in Figure 29 represents those who paid for those assets. In this case, equity owners paid $100 for the assets. If this were a public company, shareholders would be the ones holding the equity stake.

If the owner or owners of the company are not satisfied with a 10% return on their investment, they can increase this return by using other people's money to finance part of the assets. Figure 30 illustrates a company that is financed both by debt (other people's money) and owners' equity. In this case, $100 of Assets is financed by $25 of Debt and $75 of Equity. The left side must always equal the right side, so Assets = Liabilities + Equity.

Fig. 30: Assets financed with $25 of Debt and $75 of Equity

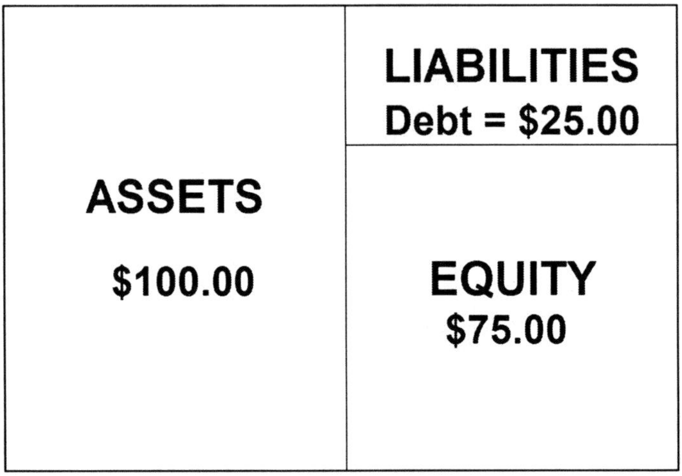

ASSETS **$100.00**	**LIABILITIES** **Debt = $25.00**
	EQUITY **$75.00**

Originally, when assets were financed only by equity, the net income was $10. When debt is employed to finance a portion of assets, the interest must be subtracted from the $10 in income to arrive at the adjusted net income because debt is not free. Assuming that the interest rate on $25 of debt is 6%, the interest expense is $1.50 ($25 x 6%).

Adjusted Net Income = $10.00 - $1.50 = $8.50

How did the return on equity increase when other people's money was used to finance a portion of assets? As a reminder, the formula for return on equity is as follows:

Return on Equity = Net Income/Equity

Before the calculation, it is important to notice that equity is no longer $100 as it was in the previous example. We used $25 of other people's money, and therefore, equity is only $75. The return on equity is as follows:

Return on Equity = $8.50/$75.00 = 11.33%

The return on equity increased from 10.00% to 11.33%. This is an illustration of positive financial leverage. When no debt was used, the business was returning 10%. For discussion purposes we will refer to it as a 10%-Return-Business. Borrowing at 6% against a 10%-Return-Business generates a positive financial leverage that increases the return on equity. If the cost of debt were higher than 10%, negative financial leverage would have decreased return on equity. It is not advisable to borrow at 12% against a 10%-Return-Business.

An example of a company that uses even more debt in its capital structure is illustrated in Figure 31. In this example, $100 in Assets is financed with $75 of Debt and only $25 of Equity.

Fig. 31: Assets financed with $75 of Debt and $25 of Equity

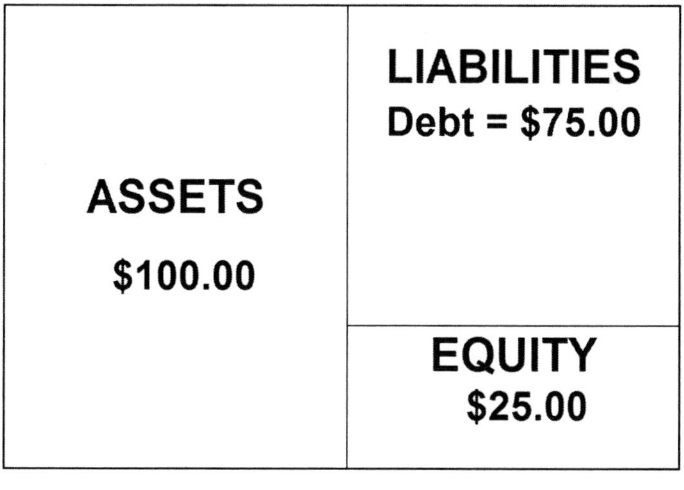

Because the cost of debt is still 6%, the interest expense on $75 of Debt is $4.50. Remember that originally, net income was $10 when no debt was employed. Net income must be reduced by the cost of debt.

Net Income = $10.00 - $4.50 = $5.50

To calculate the return on equity, net income is divided by equity, which in this case is $25.

Return on Equity = $5.50/$25.00 = 22.00%

Note that the higher the proportion of debt that is used to finance assets, the higher the return on equity. However, this only happens in this example when the cost of debt is less than 10%. If the cost of debt were more than 10%, the negative financial leverage would cause the return on equity to decline.

How high could the return on equity be if $100 of Assets is financed by $99 of Debt and only $1 of Equity, assuming the cost of debt is still 6%?

Interest Expense: $99 x 6% = $5.94

Net Income: $10.00 - $5.94 = $4.06

Return on Equity: $4.06/$1.00 = 406%

A 406% return on equity is incredible, and it would be tempting to operate all companies with 99% debt to get this kind of return. Real estate investors usually leverage 80%, but it is not uncommon to see the leverage reach 90% to 95%.

But there is a catch to high leverage. As the debt level increases, so does the interest expense. Leverage works very well when business is great. But when business slows down due to an economic downturn or unexpected increases in expenses, companies are in a vulnerable position to weather the negative impact. Leverage is a double-edged sword. During good times, it creates great returns, but in bad times it can wipe out equity quickly. When interest payments are so high that total expenses exceed revenues, there is not enough money to operate the business. Not making interest payments may force the company into bankruptcy.

Companies with stable earnings and revenues are better positioned to afford more debt than companies in cyclical industries. Interest payments are fixed, and when earnings fluctuate as much as they do in cyclical companies, it may be difficult to make those payments.

Leverage and Trading

Borrowed money can be used to increase returns for all types of business operations. Individual traders and big brokerage companies can use leverage in their trading activities. As mentioned before, leverage can be detrimental when things do not turn out the way they were intended. For example, if a stock trader, Joe, buys $50,000 worth of securities with cash on hand (not borrowed), his balance sheet will look like the one shown in Figure 32.

Fig. 32: Joe uses no debt

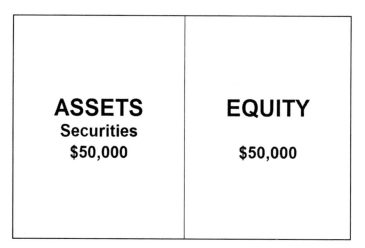

If things go his way, and the price of securities increases by 3% in one day, he will make $1,500. Assets and equity will both reach $51,500. But if things do not go as planned and the price of securities decreases by 3%, assets and equity will both decrease to $48,500. Joe will be disappointed, but he will still have most of his equity.

Since Joe is convinced that the first scenario will happen, he decides to max out all of his credit cards, take out a home equity loan, and borrow against his business. He borrows a total of $1,700,000. In this scenario, he now has $1,750,000 to invest, including his initial $50,000 equity. His balance sheet is shown in Figure 33.

Fig. 33: Joe uses debt

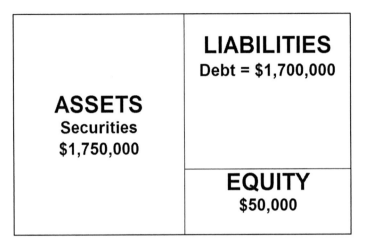

Joe buys $1,750,000 worth of securities that he intends to hold for one to five days, then sell and cash out. Suppose that his projections are right and the price of his holdings increases by 3%. Figure 34 illustrates this change.

Fig. 34: Joe's investments gain 3%

Although the price of his securities only increases by 3%, Joe more than doubles his money (his equity). He can sell the securities for $1,802,500, pay off the loan of $1,700,000, and still have $102,500 (the difference between $1,802,500 and $1,700,000). Because he originally invested $50,000 of his money, he nets $52,500.

What happens if things do not go his way? What if instead of increasing in price, the price of his holdings decreases by 3%? His new balance sheet is shown in Figure 35.

Fig. 35: Joe's investments lose 3%

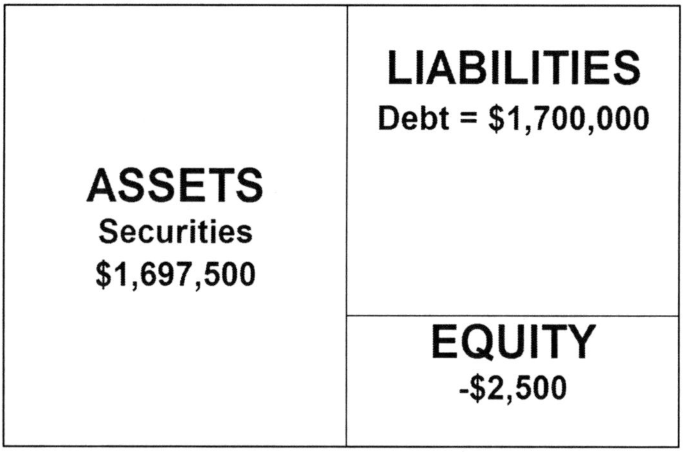

ASSETS Securities $1,697,500	LIABILITIES Debt = $1,700,000
	EQUITY -$2,500

A slight movement of prices in the wrong direction wipes out more than his entire equity. His holdings decrease by $52,500 ($1,750,000 x 3%). If he were to sell the securities, he would receive only $1,697,500. This would not be enough to even pay off the $1,700,000 loan: he would have to cover the difference from his own pocket. Not only would he have to pay $2,500 ($1,700,000 - $1,697,500) to pay off the loan, he would also lose the original $50,000 in equity.

Because Joe is sure of his prediction, he decides to hold on to his investments a little longer instead of selling when the market dropped 3%. However, negative economic news is released and the price of his holdings decreases by an additional 10%. Now, his balance sheet is shown in Figure 36.

Fig. 36: Joe's investments tumble

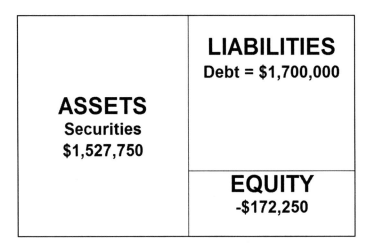

To possibly avoid additional losses, Joe sells the securities. He receives $1,527,750 from the sale. In addition to being $172,250 short to pay off the $1,700,000 loan, he lost $50,000 in his original equity. His total loss is $222,250. Because he does not have $172,250 to pay off the loan, creditors foreclose on his house and take his business. For Joe, the game is over. He gambled and lost.

How Much Debt is Too Much?

It is relatively easy to check how much debt a public company carries by looking at its balance sheet. Because assets must equal liabilities plus shareholders' equity, investors can quickly calculate a ratio of liabilities to assets. This shows investors the percentage of assets that are financed by liabilities.

Excellent companies tend to carry less debt and spend a smaller portion of revenues on interest payments compared to mediocre companies. Good businesses are so profitable that they do not need to borrow much money. Instead, they generate so much cash that they are able to finance operations and future growth internally.

A good way to understand this concept is to visualize ourselves as a business. We must generate enough income to finance our personal expenses, or in other words, the operation of our lives. If we make a significant amount of money, we have little or no need to borrow. Whatever is left after expenses can be saved or invested. If we do not generate enough money to cover our expenses, we might have to borrow and go into debt.

There is no single ratio that can tell investors how much debt is too much because each industry is different. The best way to make this judgment is to compare a company's debt level to those of its competitors. Usually, the company with the least amount of debt is likely to be the strongest competitor.

Examples of Leverage Destruction

Leverage can boost returns if things go well and destroy returns when they go the opposite way. The examples below illustrate companies that used leverage to their destruction.

Long-Term Capital Management

Long-Term Capital Management (LTMC) was a U.S. hedge fund founded in 1994 by John Meriwether, the former vice-chairman and head of bond trading at Salomon Brothers. He recruited two Nobel Prize winners in economics, Myron S. Scholes and Robert C. Merton, and a former Harvard University economics professor and retired vice-chairman of the Federal Reserve Board of Governors, David W. Mullins, Jr. The fund had a total of 12 partners. It started with $1 billion in equity and more than $100 billion of borrowed money. It used trading strategies such as fixed income arbitrage, statistical arbitrage, and pairs trading, which are all beyond the scope of this book. The idea was to find very small inefficiencies in the market. Because the inefficiencies were so small, high leverage was used to increase returns. When everything was going well, the fund was generating 40% returns per year after fees. But when things did not go as expected, the fund lost a lot of money.

Because of the Russian financial crisis in 1998, the Russian government defaulted on their government bonds. Fearing more defaults, investors panicked and sold their Japanese and European bonds in order to buy U.S. treasury bonds. The inefficiencies that were supposed to be turned into profits from differences between the prices of bonds turned into huge losses. The Federal Reserve Bank of New York had to intervene and bail out LTMC with $3.6 billion in order to avoid a collapse of the entire financial system. The total losses were $4.6 billion.

Fannie Mae and Freddie Mac

Fannie Mae and Freddie Mac were established as publicly held companies to provide liquidity to the mortgage market. The companies would buy mortgages from lenders and resell them to investors. Fannie Mae and Freddie Mac were supposed to act as pass-through entities. But because the government backed them, they were able to borrow money more cheaply than anyone else. As a result, instead of passing on some of these mortgages to investors, Fannie Mae and Freddie Mac held the mortgages on their books. They made money on the spread between what they were receiving from homeowners and what they were paying their creditors. The companies borrowed so heavily compared to their equity that when only a small percentage of homeowners defaulted, losses mounted. In the end, the government had to bail them out, but shareholders of Fannie Mae and Freddie Mac stock were almost entirely wiped out. Some investors believed that Fannie Mae and Freddie Mac were too big to fail and that the government would not allow them to go down. They were right because both of the companies are still in existence, but shareholders are left with almost nothing because the government took over the majority of the ownership stake. Figures 37 and 38 illustrate the collapses of Fannie Mae and Freddie Mac stock prices respectively.

Fig. 37: Fannie Mae Stock Price Collapse

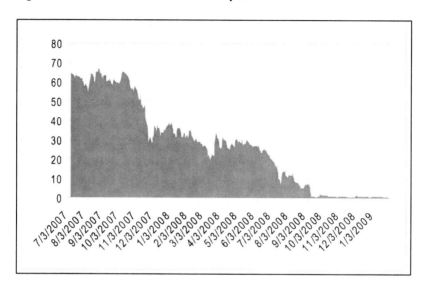

Fig. 38: Freddie Mac Stock Price Collapse

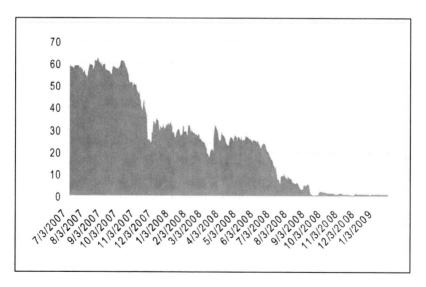

American International Group - AIG

AIG is a large American insurance corporation headquartered in New York City. It provides insurance and financial services worldwide. The company got into trouble by getting involved in the derivative business—specifically, *credit default swaps*. These are instruments that expose a company to a potential liability.

A credit default swap is an agreement between two parties. The buyer makes payments to the seller in return for protection or insurance against a default on a financial instrument the buyer holds. If the underlying security such as a bond or loan defaults, the buyer gets a payoff from the seller. For example, a bank wishes to make a loan to a corporation, but is concerned about the default risk. A company, such as AIG, assumes the default risk and takes on the potential liability in exchange for periodic payments. When making such guarantees to hundreds or thousands of companies, and assuming that a small percentage (perhaps 4.0%) will default, the company can determine how high the periodic payments need to be to generate a worthwhile profit.

Because this type of business was extremely profitable before 2008, it attracted other companies who competed for the same business. The only way to get more business was to charge less than the competition, which meant making more aggressive assumptions on the probability of defaults. Instead of 4.0%, the company might have assumed that 3.0% or 3.5% of companies will default. This is fine when defaults stay within the assumptions, but once the percentage of defaults surpasses this range, someone has to assume the losses. If the companies guaranteeing default losses could not cover them, they would go bankrupt, and the companies on the other side of the contract that were counting on the payoffs would be forced to take the losses. This is equivalent to getting into an accident and having the insurance company not cover the damages.

AIG sold a high volume of credit default swaps that insured close to a half a trillion dollars worth of securities. The potential liability for AIG was so great that it was beyond their capacity to fulfill their obligations if things went wrong. The buyers of these instruments were banks and corporations all over the world. If AIG defaulted, all these companies would have to write down huge losses. No one knew just how detrimental it could be to the financial system and global economy if this happened.

As the economy was declining in 2008, defaults were increasing and AIG was not able to meet its obligations. The Federal Reserve made a determination that it could not allow AIG to fail and go bankrupt because of its connection to all these other institutions. Subsequently, the Fed bailed out AIG. What happened to AIG's shareholders? See Figure 39 below.

Fig. 39: AIG Stock Price Collapse

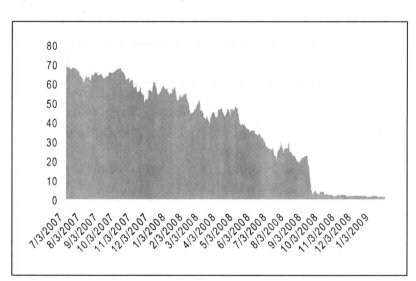

This major American insurance corporation destroyed almost 100% of its shareholders' wealth within one year. It only took one strategic mistake. This destruction was possible because of the abuse of leverage.

Return on Equity

Companies that can generate a high return on equity without overleveraging are preferred over ones that generate a low return on equity. But the valuation model we introduced in Chapter

5 does not account for the return on equity. It accounts for the discount rate, earnings growth, and the terminal sale price. Why is it important to invest in companies with a high return on equity? There is a correlation between the return on equity and earnings growth (one variable in the valuation model).

Every year earnings not paid out as dividends become part of equity. Remember that earnings are internally generated equity. For example, if a business that was started with $100 in equity generated $20 in earnings, its return on original equity is 20% ($20/$100). The $20 of earnings is added to the original $100 in equity, resulting in $120 of equity. In order for the company to maintain the 20% return on equity, it has to reinvest this additional $20 at a rate of 20%. If the company simply places this $20 in the bank at 2% and fails to reinvest it at 20%, the future return on equity will decline. So it is fair to assume that when the company maintains high returns on equity for years, it is reinvesting its earnings at high rates. And when earnings are reinvested at high rates, this creates earnings growth that increases the value of the company and makes investors wealthier every year.

It is possible to predict future earnings using the return on equity in the following manner.

Earnings Growth = Return on Equity x % Retained Earnings

Earnings growth is calculated by multiplying the return on equity times the percentage of retained earnings. As mentioned before, the only earnings that are added to the equity are earnings that were not paid out in dividends. Two scenarios show earnings growth calculations. Scenario #1 assumes that 100% of earnings are retained. Scenario #2 assumes that 60% of earnings are retained and 40% are paid out in dividends. To do the calculations above, we are only interested in the retained portion of earnings because this is the portion that has to be reinvested to maintain return on equity.

Scenario #1

Return on Equity: 20%
Net Income: $10
Net Income Retained: $10 or 100% retained ($10/$10)
Dividends: $0
Earnings Growth: 20% x 100% = 20%

It can be assumed that the company is likely to grow earnings at 20%.

Scenario #2

Return on Equity: 20%
Net Income: $10
Net Income Retained: $6 or 60% retained ($6/$10)
Dividends: $4
Earnings Growth: 20% x 60% = 12%

It can be assumed that the company is likely to grow earnings at 12%.

Efficiency Test

Investors can quickly determine whether the management is reinvesting retained earnings efficiently. Figure 40 illustrates this concept. The data shown in Figure 40 may be found from sources such as the Value Line Investment Survey that is discussed in Chapter 10.

Fig. 40: Efficient Reinvestment of Retained Earnings

Year	Earnings Per Share	Dividends	Retained
1999	$1.10	$0.33	$0.77
2000	$1.38	$0.41	$0.96
2001	$1.36	$0.41	$0.95
2002	$1.43	$0.43	$1.00
2003	$2.07	$0.62	$1.45
2004	$2.01	$0.60	$1.41
2005	$2.21	$0.66	$1.55
2006	$2.50	$0.75	$1.75
2007	$2.70	$0.81	$1.89
2008	$3.24	$0.97	$2.27
Total			$14.00

In our example, earnings per share were $1.10 in 1999 and $3.24 in 2008. The increase is $2.14 ($3.24 - $1.10). Did the management do a good job of allocating capital? It depends on the cost to increase these earnings. The total of all the retained earnings is $14.00; this represents the cost. The benefit is the increase in earnings per share, which is $2.14. Divide the benefit by the cost to determine the return on the retained earnings.

Return on Retained Earnings = $2.14/$14.00 = 15.29%

At 15.29%, it can be concluded that the retained earnings have been employed by the management efficiently to increase earnings per share. Figure 41 shows another example.

Fig. 41: Inefficient Reinvestment of Retained Earnings

Year	Earnings Per Share	Dividends	Retained
1999	$1.10	$0.33	$0.77
2000	$1.11	$0.33	$0.78
2001	$1.14	$0.34	$0.80
2002	$1.00	$0.30	$0.70
2003	$1.16	$0.35	$0.81
2004	$1.18	$0.35	$0.83
2005	$1.20	$0.36	$0.84
2006	$1.17	$0.35	$0.82
2007	$1.25	$0.38	$0.88
2008	$1.35	$0.41	$0.95
Total			$8.16

In 1999, earnings per share were $1.10, and in 2008, they were $1.35. The increase in earnings per share is $0.25 ($1.35 - $1.10). Did the management do a good job of allocating capital? The total of all the earnings retained, $8.16, represents the cost. The benefit is the increase in earnings per share, which is $0.25. Once again, divide the benefit by the cost to determine the return on the retained earnings.

Return on Retained Earnings = $0.25/$8.16 = 3.06%

At 3.06%, it can be concluded that the retained earnings have not been employed by the management efficiently to increase earnings per share.

Conclusion

Every business has assets, liabilities, and equity. By reviewing the financial statements, investors can quickly determine whether the company has too much debt and if the management employed capital at satisfactory rates.

Chapter 7

DIVERSIFICATION

DIVERSIFICATION

Diversification refers to investing funds in a variety of different securities and asset classes. Its purpose is to help investors minimize risk. However, at the same time diversification also minimizes the chances of above average returns. Many mutual funds own close to 100 investments in their portfolios. If a fund manager makes a wise stock selection, and the price of an individual stock doubles, the net effect on the portfolio is 1%. But at the same time, if a company in which the manager has invested goes out of business, the portfolio only loses 1%. Some investors spread their money across too many stocks without understanding the companies they are buying. As Warren Buffett says, diversification protects investors from their own ignorance.

A broad diversification approach does not give any incentive for finding undervalued companies because, as explained above, good picks do not have much effect when a portfolio has 100 stocks. Also, a portfolio with so many stocks will not perform much differently than the Standards and Poor's (S&P) 500 or other broad indexes.

Thus, broad diversification does not make much sense from a perspective of maximizing returns. However, neither does placing all available money into one investment. Some investors are more comfortable with having more concentrated portfolios than others. If an investor can only find six or seven excellent picks in different industries, it does not make much sense to place money in companies with poor to average returns simply for the sake of diversification. These stocks will be a drag on the returns from the good picks. Also, it is important to realize that some companies have different product mixes that serve different clientele. This means that there is a certain amount of diversification within the companies themselves.

A basketball coach will only play the best players. He or she will not play the entire team just because everyone should get a chance to play. Why would an investor need to play 100 stocks all at once if only 7 are worth keeping? Maybe this is because he or she does not know which of the 100 picks represent the best seven stocks. In that case, he or she should not be picking individual stocks, but should be investing in index funds or letting someone else manage the money.

Jim Cramer of *Mad Money* recommends that investors spend one hour per week per stock following each investment. A portfolio of ten stocks would require about ten hours per week. Obviously, this investment of time would make it difficult to keep track of 50 stocks.

Warren Buffett advocated that investors be given a punch card with 20 punches for a lifetime. Every time an investment is made, a hole is punched in the card. By following this method, investors would be forced to think hard about what they are doing and only invest in the very best opportunities.

Conclusion

The goal of investing is maximizing returns and minimizing risks. Buying five stocks that are expected to grow 20% is better than placing 100% of one's investment funds into one stock that is expected to grow 20%. Buying fifty stocks out of which five are expected to grow 20% and the rest are expected to grow only 5% is not the best use of investment dollars. Just buy the ones that have the best investment potential.

Chapter 8

ECONOMY

ECONOMY

As the world entered a severe recession in December 2007, politicians, reporters, investors, and the general public began pointing fingers at various individuals and organizations in an attempt to identify the culprits who created all the misery. People lost their homes, factories shut down, unemployment headed toward double-digit figures, banks became insolvent, and the stock market crashed. Some thought we were going into a depression, and others proclaimed it to be the worst time since the Great Depression.

What is amazing is that everyone was surprised that the world was experiencing an economic downturn. No one seems to remember that recessions have been around for decades. It is a fact of life that the economy will go through periods of expansion followed by periods of contraction. The concept of business cycles is illustrated in Figure 42.

Fig. 42: The Business Cycle

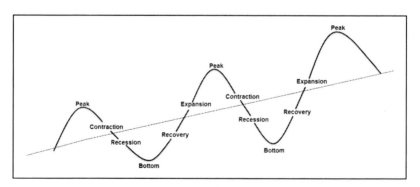

Expansion/Recovery

During the expansion and recovery stages, the demand for products and services grows. Businesses expand production to meet the demand. As production increases, businesses have to hire more people and open more factories. As unemployment declines, people have more money to spend on cars, houses, clothes, and recreational activities.

To fuel the expansion even more, banks step in to provide more credit. Spending supported by borrowed funds accelerates the expansion to a new level. Businesses borrow to expand production and consumers borrow to consume more. Home prices and common stock prices rise.

Boom/Peak

As banks run out of good prospects and search for growth opportunities, they start relaxing their underwriting criteria. To get more business, they start cutting interest rates to razor-thin levels above the interest rates they pay on deposits, and they extend credit to less creditworthy customers. Demand now becomes completely dependent on credit availability.

Contraction/Recession

The less creditworthy borrowers start defaulting on their loans. Banks are forced to take losses and curtail lending money. Once consumers have less access to credit, demand falls, and the contraction phase begins. Production now exceeds demand. Businesses have to cut back and decrease production. They stop investing in equipment and factories, and they stop hiring.

As the contraction continues, businesses reduce the number of employees. Unemployment rises and overall consumer spending declines. Businesses that borrowed heavily to grow production during the expansion face difficult times and start defaulting on their loans. People who lose their jobs default on their cars, homes, and credit card loans. Banks faced with more foreclosures further restrict lending in order to cover loan losses. Demand declines even further.

As the phase continues, overleveraged consumers and businesses file for bankruptcy. Wealth is destroyed and lives are ruined. Banks with bad loans on their books become insolvent (liabilities exceed assets), and the government takes control and sells them off in pieces. Home prices and common stock prices fall.

Trough/Bottom

Consumers and businesses are forced to deleverage and pay down the debt level. Production is cut to match demand. Lower debt burden and low interest rates encourage more borrowing, increasing the demand again. The expansion phase begins again.

Taking Advantage of the Inevitable

The economy will cycle through these phases whether the government, businesses, or investors like it or not. As much as everyone hates recessions, they are an inevitable part of capitalism. What is amazing is that people are surprised when contractions happen, and they start looking for somebody to blame. History repeats itself, but few seem to learn from it.

Instead of being surprised and blaming someone for the next recession, it is better to realize that it will happen and take advantage of it when it does. The question that investors should ask themselves is:

When is it best to <u>own</u> a great company—in good times or bad times?

Of course it is better to <u>own</u> a great company during good times because this is when a majority of companies are able to make money. The problem is that the majority of investors think along these same lines and when this happens everyone wants to own stocks. From basic economics, when the demand for something increases and the supply is stable, prices rise. When everyone wants to be in stocks, prices are high. This brings us to the next question,

When is one more likely to <u>buy</u> a great company at a reasonable price—in good times or bad times?

As mentioned above, during good times everyone wants to be in stocks, so the chances of getting good deals on excellent companies are slim. But during bad times, investors are afraid to buy, and the likelihood of buying great companies at reasonable prices is high. When the demand for stocks falls and the supply stays the same, prices fall. The majority of investors stay on the sidelines waiting for things to improve.

During the 2008-09 recession, the recreational vehicle (RV) industry went through the hardest times in the industry's history. The lack of credit availability made it difficult for customers to purchase RVs. The main three manufacturers were Fleetwood Enterprises, Winnebago Industries, and Thor Industries. All three struggled.

Fleetwood Enterprise's stock price decreased from $15.00 to $0.88 in five years. Winnebago Industries' stock price decreased from $40.00 to $4.15 in four years. Thor Industries' stock price decreased from the high of $55.00 to $11.00 in two years.

Some investigation reveals that Thor Industries was in the best position to weather the recession. It had the strongest balance sheet and no debt. For years, the management's philosophy was to carry no debt and take advantage of overleveraged competitors during contractions and recessions. The product mix was comprised mainly of towable RVs and buses. If a company like Thor is able to stay in business during a recession, the stock price is likely to appreciate upon the economic recovery.

Fleetwood Enterprises, on the other hand, was swimming in debt. Winnebago Industries had a less favorable product mix that focused mainly on large motor homes that were the hardest to finance.

Investors can also take advantage of recessions by buying *defensive* companies whose sales and earnings remain relatively stable during recessionary periods. These are the companies that sell products or services that have to be consumed during bad and good times. For example, people have to buy products such as food, toilet paper, and toothpaste no matter how the economy is performing. The stocks of these companies might decline somewhat during recessions, but they will not decrease as much as stocks of *cyclical* companies that are sensitive to business or economic cycles.

McDonald's Corporation is an example of a defensive stock. As Figure 43 below shows, its stock price was not affected at all during the recession. When people have less money, they tend to go to McDonald's instead of more expensive restaurants.

Fig. 43: McDonald's Corporation (MCD)

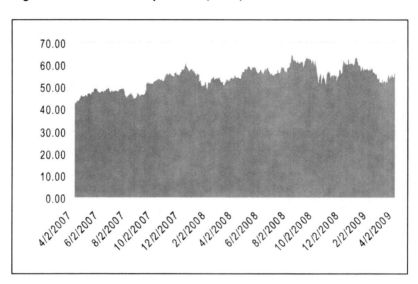

Not all defensive companies are able to keep their stock prices up as well as McDonald's in severe recessions. The point is that defensive companies will decline less than cyclical companies. If defensive companies decline far enough below their intrinsic value, they should be purchased. If they do not, investors purchasing them should not expect to earn above-average returns.

Conclusion

The economy will always go through business cycles regardless of what anyone says or how optimistic the market becomes. Hoping "this time it's different" is wishful thinking. Phases of business cycles vary in intensity and length and are difficult to predict. Rather than fearing recessions, investors can take advantage of them.

Chapter 9

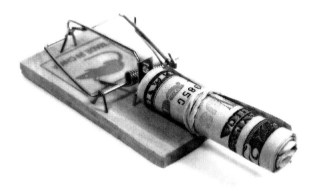

INVESTING IN IPOS

INVESTING IN IPOS

An Initial Public Offering (IPO) is a process that private companies use to sell their shares to the public so that these shares can be traded on the exchanges. Many investors think that searching for the next Microsoft is the key to riches. Unfortunately, no one tells them about all the failed IPOs.

Before investors jump on the next IPO, they should know how the odds are stacked against them. The first thing to be aware of is that IPOs are used to repay and cash out the previous financial backers. Because stocks are vehicles to own underlying businesses, a company going public must have an existing business. That business had to be financed by someone in order to get it off the ground. In a few instances, the founders may have had all the funding required, but in most cases there were private investors or venture capital firms backing them. After risking capital on a start-up, these investors want to be repaid, and an IPO is the vehicle for the sale.

Just as a person who is selling a house wants top dollar, these private backers want to sell the company for the highest possible price. They hire brokers, called underwriters, who work for investment banks. Together with the underwriters, they set the price. A tremendous marketing effort is employed, creating the hype needed to get the highest possible price. It is unlikely for the average investor to get a reasonable price in this environment because the price is not set by the bids of buyers and sellers. That's why many refer to an IPO as "It's Probably Overpriced."

Investors mistakenly believe that underwriters act in the best interest of investors by pitching them a new IPO and allowing them to get in at a low price before the stock takes off on the open market. Just as a homebuyer should not be confused about whom the listing agent represents, investors need to recognize the fact that underwriters are paid by the sellers whom they actually represent. No seller would approach the underwriter saying, "Mr. Underwriter, I have a business to sell to the public, but I would like to sell it for 60% of what it is worth because I feel generous today." Usually, it's the opposite. Sellers have unrealistic pricing expectations, and the underwriters have to bring them down to reality.

Just as a homeowner would not be eager to sell a house in a bad market, a business owner will not be eager to sell a business in a bad market. Initial public offerings are timed properly to sell in the most favorable market for the sellers. It is no coincidence that IPO activity dries up during bear markets. The only sellers taking their companies public are the ones that absolutely have to sell. Otherwise, they will wait for the market to recover.

Conclusion

With the odds stacked against investors, it is better to wait for a company to trade on the open market for some time before buying shares. Private sellers and underwriters have a pretty good idea what the business is worth and when to sell it. They will not cut anyone a deal, but the stock market consisting of millions buyers and sellers will. Investors should stay away from most IPOs. Instead, they should buy good companies in bad markets when everyone else is selling, and sell in good markets when everyone else is buying. Unfortunately, most investors do the opposite.

Chapter 10

ANALYZING INVESTMENTS

ANALYZING INVESTMENTS

The goal of analyzing an investment is to decide if the investment should be purchased at the price being offered.

Step #1: Perform a Quick Analysis

Before investing the time and effort to analyze a company in great detail, investors can review a company's printout from Value Line Investment Survey, paying attention to the return on equity and earnings growth. Other preliminary sources of information available online include Yahoo Finance, MSN Money, and Google Finance.

Value Line tracks approximately 1,700 stocks in over 90 industries, publishes reports four times a year, and publishes weekly full-page reports on approximately 130 stocks. While an annual subscription is available to individual investors, you may be able to access the online version through your public library.

The Value Line Ratings and Reports (R&R) sheets contain a wealth of information, including records such as the earnings per share for several years, depending on the company.

If preliminary research shows that earnings per share are trending up and returns on equity are high (above 15%), it is appropriate to move to the next step, a quick valuation.

Step #2: Perform a Quick Valuation

Investors can waste an enormous amount of time analyzing an overpriced company. It is smart to quickly look at the P/E ratio or the price range within the previous 52 weeks to get an idea if there is a possibility of undervaluation. For example, if a company usually trades at P/E ratios of 16 to 25 and is currently trading at a P/E of 13, further analysis is appropriate. However, if it is trading at a P/E ratio of 60, it is unlikely that it is priced fairly. Investors can also enter a few variables into the valuation model discussed in Chapter 5 and monitor the valuation results.

All of the data needed for the valuation model is available from the Value Line R&R charts.

Step #3: Study the Company and the Industry

The SEC requires public companies to provide certain information. Quarterly and annual reports, plus proxy statements, are available through company websites, usually under the investment relations section. Investors should always read the reports to familiarize themselves with the business before they invest. In the reports, the management discusses the business, competition, risks, and compensation. Consolidated financial statements are also provided, including the income statement, balance sheet, and the statement of cash flows.

It is important to understand the industry in which a company operates. Some industries are easier to understand than others; some are more competitive than others; some are more regulated than others. By studying an industry, investors will understand the individual companies better. Once again, we can call on the wisdom of Warren Buffett who has stated that he finds it important to stay within his "circle of competence" and only invest in businesses that he understands.

Reading books or articles on particular industries or companies makes it easier to understand annual and quarterly reports of particular companies. A tremendous amount of information regarding industries is available in libraries.

The Internet is a great source for information, too. One website, www.glassdoor.com, provides information about what current or former employees are saying about their companies. Comments are divided into pros and cons. There will always be employees dissatisfied with any company, and negative comments should not always stop anyone from investing. Nevertheless, sometimes employees might say something so important that investors should take notice. For example, a publicly traded consulting company has unusually high employee turnover. Employee comments reveal that the management mistreats its employees. One comment stated that pleasing Wall Street is of paramount importance to the management who holds stock options. This one comment should make investors beware because management should be more concerned about operating the business and less concerned with the daily fluctuations in the stock price. If management does a good job, the stock price will take care of itself. It is not unheard of for companies to "cook the books" to please Wall Street. If they cannot treat their employees with respect, why should investors think that they would be treated any differently? This is a red flag.

Another example of useful information from www. glassdoor.com is about a well-known investment research company. By reading the comments, investors learned that employees are happy working for the company, but a large number think that they are underpaid compared to other firms. This type of information might not stop anyone from investing in the company, but it is useful to know.

Step #4: Answer the Questions

After studying a company and its industry, investors should be able to answer the following questions:

1) Does the business possess a moat or a competitive advantage?

2) Is the moat sustainable and durable?

3) Is it likely that the company will be around in 10 years?

4) Is the company in an industry that is changing rapidly, or is it in an industry that is stable?

5) Is the business simple and easy to understand?

6) Is the business run by managers who reinvest earnings at high rates of return?

7) Is it likely that the business will keep generating high returns on equity?

8) Is the stock being sold at a favorable price?

Step #5: Purchase Shares or Move On

If the analysis indicates it's a good business that is priced favorably, shares should be purchased. Otherwise, investors should move on to other investment alternatives.

Conclusion

Value Line is a great source that allows investors to quickly review a company and decide if further investigation is warranted. Annual and quarterly reports about particular companies are important, but they are written by the management and may present a biased view. Articles and books written about companies and industries provide a great deal of information and are often written by outsiders who may or may not be biased. However, insiders also write books. So pay attention to who is the author and consider their motivation when determining the value of the information.

Analyzing investments, especially when companies are easy to understand, is not very difficult, but it requires work. The more investors know about particular investments, the more they will have an advantage over other market participants. When the market panics, investors can assess whether the reaction is appropriate or if it presents a buying opportunity.

Chapter11

WHEN TO SELL

WHEN TO SELL

Parting with an investment can be more difficult than purchasing it. Before discussing when to sell, investors would benefit from first learning when NOT to sell.

Selling a stock based solely on the fact that its price went down is not a good reason. If everything else stays the same, this decrease in price is a buying opportunity. If the stock is already in one's portfolio, this is an opportunity to add more shares.

The best time to sell is when projections turn out positive, the company prospers well, and the market realizes its full value by pricing it correctly. This is the scenario that investors hope for when making investments. There may be times when the market gets overexcited and sees nothing but an overly positive outlook for stocks in general or for the stocks of individual companies. This tends to result in overpricing and presents the perfect time to sell. An excellent example of this behavior occurred during the dot-com bubble from 1995 to 2001.

Another reason to sell is when an investor finds a better investment opportunity. Selling a stock that is 20% undervalued in order to purchase a stock that is 60% undervalued is a legitimate reason.

Sometimes investors need to take a loss because they realize they originally made a mistake in evaluating a company or something deteriorated permanently since the analysis. If after three years the stock does not recover, maybe it is time to move on. Keeping the money in a losing position in hopes of a rebound is not advisable. This money can be put to work in other investments. Mistakes are part of investing. The goal is to make enough money on good investments to far outweigh the losses on bad investments and to learn from one's mistakes to become a better investor over time.

The final reason to sell is to take a tax deduction and repurchase the stock after an allowable period under the wash sale rule. If the investment decreases in price, the IRS allows realized investment losses to be offset against investment gains.

The IRS also allows capital losses up to a certain amount per year to be deducted against ordinary income. Investors should consult their accountants for details about the wash sale rule.

Conclusion

Selling decisions may be difficult, especially when things do not turn out as planned. Ego and the denial of the possibility of failure may interfere. Mistakes are part of life and investing. It is better to assume that mistakes will happen and have the discipline and preparation to act when they do.

Chapter 12

CASE STUDIES

CASE STUDIES

This chapter illustrates the analysis of four excellent companies. All of these companies were considered for the portfolios of Classic Value Investors, LLC, and three of them were purchased.

Case Study #1–Burlington Northern Santa Fe (BNI)

Burlington Northern Santa Fe is one of the seven main North American freight railroads that handle 90% of the freight traffic in the US. The company's earnings per share have gone from $1.00 in 1992 to $6.40 in 2008. The returns on equity ranged from 9.1% to 17.9% between 1998 and 2008. An investor who invested $10,000 in 1997 at a price of $25 per share would have $45,840 in 2008, assuming a price of $114. That's an annual return of 14.85% excluding dividends.

The Railroad Industry

The railroad industry is important to the American economy. As the population grows, the demand for transportation services increases, and so does the need to move raw materials, food, and finished products. According to the Association of American Railroads, America's railroads are the most efficient and cost-effective in the world. Because of this affordability, finished products such as food, clothes, and electricity generated from coal cost much less than they otherwise would. On average, moving goods by rail is three or more times more fuel efficient than by truck.

According to the U.S. Department of Transportation (DOT), the U.S. freight railroad demand is anticipated to increase 88% by 2035. At the current rate of rail construction, demand will outpace supply, pushing the rates up. Railroads are a regulated industry, and companies have to be careful how much they raise rates. They wish to avoid being considered in possession of too much market power. Unlike public roads that are maintained by the government, private railroads maintain their own infrastructure. Maintaining the infrastructure is in the best interest of the government and the public. Therefore, regulators have to let railroads raise rates high enough to be profitable and have enough money to spend on infrastructure.

Moat or Competitive Advantage

Burlington Northern Santa Fe enjoys a competitive advantage that comes from network effect and low cost structure.

Network Effect: Each railroad company has a rail network that allows goods to reach their destinations. The bigger the network, the more shippers want to use it. Because of the high cost and the challenge of obtaining rights-of-way associated with building such networks, railroad companies are protected by these huge costs of entry. The protection that the companies enjoy allows them to maintain profitability.

Low Cost Structure: Not only are railroads more efficient than other transportation options, they require fewer employees to transport goods. Transporting a 9,000-foot, 300-car train requires only two train employees. To transport the same amount of freight by trucks requires 300 or more drivers. The lower labor cost structure that railroads enjoy over other transportation options allows railroads to undercut the competition and still make good profits. Many trucking companies even use rail transportation themselves to cut costs. United Parcel Service (UPS) is a major consumer of railroads. Shippers select transportation options based on service and price. Burlington Northern Santa Fe has the lowest average total cost of the seven major railroads in North America.

First Quarter 2009

When the economy goes through a recession, there is less need for transportation and profits are lower. As a result, the price of Burlington Northern Santa Fe fell from its high of $114.60

in 2008 to $50.86 in the First Quarter 2009, which is a decrease of more than 50%.

Analysis

Figure 44 contains conservative assumptions of a 10% growth rate for the next 10 years and a terminal P/E ratio of 15. These assumptions conclude that the stock is worth approximately $107.78 per share. At $50.86 per share, it is equivalent to purchasing $1.00 in value for $0.47 or getting almost a 53% discount to value.

Fig. 44: Valuation of Burlington Northern Santa Fe

FACTS	VARIABLES	VALUE CALCULATIONS				
Current Trading Price	$50.86		Year	Projected Earnings	Payout Ratio	Dividends	Discounted Dividends
Current Earnings Per Share	$6.34	Year	Projected Earnings	Payout Ratio	Dividends	Discounted Dividends
Current P/E Ratio	8.0	1	$6.97	20%	$1.39	$1.27
Dividend Payout	20%	2	$7.67	20%	$1.53	$1.27
		3	$8.44	20%	$1.69	$1.27
ASSUMPTIONS		4	$9.28	20%	$1.86	$1.27
Earnings Growth Rate (1st Five Years)	10.00%	5	$10.21	20%	$2.04	$1.27
Earnings Growth Rate (2nd Five Years)	10.00%	6	$11.23	20%	$2.25	$1.27
Discount Rate	10.0%	7	$12.35	20%	$2.47	$1.27
P/E Ratio in 10 Years	15	8	$13.59	20%	$2.72	$1.27
		9	$14.95	20%	$2.99	$1.27
RESULTS		10	$16.44	20%	$3.29	$1.27
Value of Future Dividends Today	$12.68					$12.68
Value of Future Sales Price Today	$95.10					
Value of the Stock	$107.78	10	Projected Earnings	P/E Ratio in 10 Years	Terminal Value	Discounted Terminal Value
			$16.44	15	$246.66	$95.10
Discount to Value	**52.81%**					

With the competitive advantages railroads have over other transportation options, it allows the industry to stay profitable even in bad economic times. Our economy cannot function without railroads. Unfortunately, goods cannot be transported over the Internet. Technology can improve the operations of transportation options, but it will never take away the need to transport goods. Burlington Northern Santa Fe is an excellent investment for long-term investors.

Case Study #2 - Thor Industries (THO)

Thor Industries manufactures motor homes and travel trailers in the U.S. and Canada. In 1980, the company was founded when Wade F. B. Thompson and Peter B. Orthwein purchased Airstream, which was struggling at the time. Immediately following the acquisition, they turned the company around by improving quality, cutting costs, and strengthening dealer relationships. Since 1980, the management has had a track record of excellence in operational efficiency and capital allocation. Understanding the cyclical nature of the RV industry, the company operates with no debt. During tough times, it is able to stay in business and acquire mismanaged companies that fit into Thor's business. Just as they did with Airstream, Thor improved the operations of the newly acquired businesses and made them competitive again. The founders still own about 36% of outstanding shares, which keeps them aligned with the shareholders' interests.

An investor who purchased $10,000 worth of shares in 1998 for $5 per share would have seen the investment grow to $120,000 in 2007 if he or she sold at the top price of $60 per share.

The RV Industry

RV manufacturing companies are in the business of producing and selling recreational vehicles such as motor homes and travel trailers. People buy these vehicles for the experience and for the long-term cost savings compared to other vacationing options. The long-term trends for the RV industry are favorable because of population and demographic trends. Ownership of RVs in the US is continuously increasing. According to the Alliance for Aging Research, approximately every seven seconds another Baby Boomer turns 50. This is equivalent to 11,000 new 50-year-olds every day. This is good news for the RV industry because the typical RV owner is 49 years old. RV consumers are also the best borrowers. The delinquency rate on RV loans is lower than on other consumer loans.

Moat or Competitive Advantage

Thor Industries enjoys a competitive advantage that comes from intangible assets and network effects.

Intangible Assets: Thor Industries manufactures its products under brands such as Airstream, General Coach, Dutchmen, Four Winds, and many others. Brand names in the RV industry are important. Consumers who purchase top national brands benefit from a better resale value and more availability for replacement parts and mechanics who know how to fix problems.

Network Effects: Because most RVs are sold by independent dealers, a large network of dealers is valuable to RV manufacturers. Having a network of dealers is like having a large sales force. As of July 31, 2008, there were approximately 1,734 dealers carrying products from Thor Industries in the U.S. and Canada. Duplicating this network is not an easy task.

First Quarter 2009

Similar to other manufacturing sectors, the RV industry experienced a sharp decline in sales during the 2008-09 recession. Because RVs are typically financed by bank loans, the tightness of credit significantly affected the demand. In tough times, people still have to eat, but they don't have to buy luxury goods such as RVs. Many smaller manufacturers, especially those who took on a significant amount of debt, went out of business. Thor Industries stock declined from over $50 in October 2007 to $9.54 in the First Quarter 2009.

Analysis

Thor's earnings per share were $2.41 in 2007 and $1.66 in 2008. The company is the most likely to weather poor economic conditions, compared with other RV manufacturing companies. It has no debt and the most diversified product mix. About 80%

of their RVs are smaller towable trailers that are easier to finance. If the company stays in business and recovers its earnings to $1.65 per share over the next five years, the stock is worth over $16 per share.

Fig. 45: Valuation of Thor Industries

FACTS	VARIABLES	VALUE CALCULATIONS			
Current Trading Price	$9.54		Projected	Payout	Dividends	Discounted
Current Earnings Per Share	$0.50	Year	Earnings	Ratio		Dividends
Current P/E Ratio	19.1	1	$0.64	10%	$0.06	$0.06
Dividend Payout	10%	2	$0.81	10%	$0.08	$0.07
		3	$1.02	10%	$0.10	$0.08
ASSUMPTIONS		4	$1.30	10%	$0.13	$0.09
Earnings Growth Rate (1st Five Years)	27.00%	5	$1.65	10%	$0.17	$0.10
Earnings Growth Rate (2nd Five Years)	10.00%	6	$1.82	10%	$0.18	$0.10
Discount Rate	10.0%	7	$2.00	10%	$0.20	$0.10
P/E Ratio in 10 Years	15	8	$2.20	10%	$0.22	$0.10
		9	$2.42	10%	$0.24	$0.10
RESULTS		10	$2.66	10%	$0.27	$0.10
Value of Future Dividends Today	$0.91					$0.91
Value of Future Sales Price Today	$15.39					
Value of the Stock	$16.29	10	Projected	P/E Ratio in	Terminal	Discounted
			Earnings	10 Years	Value	Terminal Value
			$2.66	15	$39.91	$15.39
Discount to Value	41.44%					

In Figure 45, it is important to notice that the earnings per share chosen are $0.50. Based on our research and projections of other analysts, we believe this number is a good indication of earnings during the 2008-09 recession. Another important factor is the earnings growth rate of 27% for the first five years. Such a high growth rate is chosen because it is assumed that the company is able to recover earnings to the level of $1.65 in five years as shown in Year 5 in Figure 45. Since earnings were at $1.66 in 2008, it is realistic to make this assumption. The value of $16 per share is on the low end because earnings were depressed so much during the 2008-09 recession that the recovery might increase earnings faster than 27%, making the stock worth significantly more than $16 per share.

Case Study #3 – Wells Fargo & Company (WFC)

Wells Fargo & Company is a provider of retail, commercial, and corporate banking services in the United States. The company is one of the most profitable banks in the country.

The Banking Industry

Banks are in the business of selling a commodity product called money. Just as other businesses do, banks buy the raw materials for one price and resell them for a higher price. Banks mainly get their money from depositors who open a checking or savings account. People might not think of it this way, but by depositing money in the bank, the general public is simply lending money to the banks. Banks might pay 2% to depositors and then turn around and lend it to consumers or businesses for 5%.

Banks are highly leveraged institutions; for every $100 in assets, $90 is borrowed from depositors or other lenders and only $10 is in form of equity. Being leveraged so much makes banks vulnerable to economic downturns that increase loan delinquencies. Because of very thin margins, one bad loan may wipe out the profits of several good loans. A poorly managed bank can destroy shareholders' wealth quickly.

Moat or Competitive Advantage

Wells Fargo enjoys a competitive advantage that comes from switching costs and cost advantages.

Customer-Switching Costs: Banks in general enjoy a high return on equity because of high switching costs for the depositors. Switching banks is a hassle, and unless it becomes a necessity, people are not likely to switch banks.

Cost Advantages: As with any company operating in a commodity business, the company with the lowest cost structure usually earns the highest returns on capital and is the most likely to survive during tough times. Wells Fargo enjoys the widest moat in the banking industry because it possesses the lowest funding costs. Over many years, Wells Fargo's strategy has been to cross sell to its customers. On average, each customer of Wells Fargo has over five products with Wells Fargo such as a checking account, brokerage account, and credit card. Every year, the number of products each customer has is increasing, and the company's goal is to increase the average number of products to eight. Each product a customer adds increases the switching costs because the hassle of moving multiple products to another bank is more than moving one product. The cross-selling strategy generates growth internally and is difficult to duplicate on a short-term basis. Other banks such as Citigroup or Bank of America mainly grow by acquisitions, a process that is more expensive than growing internally.

Because of the high cross-sell ratio, Wells Fargo is able to pay less for its deposits than most competitors. During Fourth Quarter 2008, Wells Fargo's average cost of deposits was 0.91% compared with 1.59% for its large bank peers. An illustration of how this advantage translates into higher profits is shown below in Figure 46.

Fig. 46: Wells Fargo's Advantage

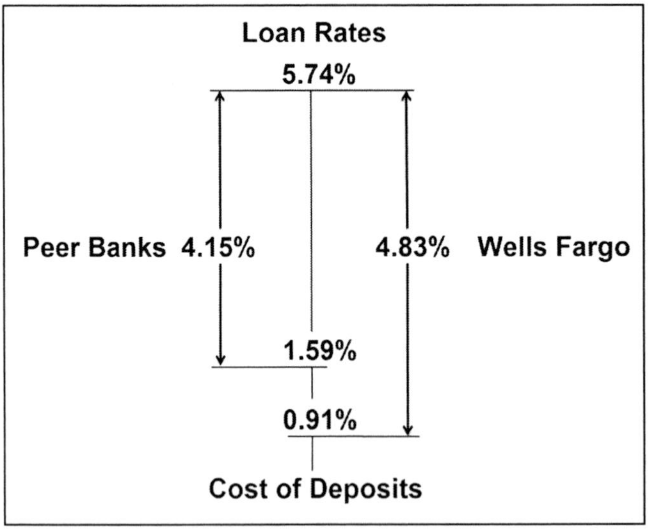

Source: 2009 Credit Suisse Financial Services Forum
Presentation by Howard Atkins, Chief Financial Officer
February 4, 2009. https://www.wellsfargo.com/invest_relations/presents

Because banks are in the commodity business, their ability to charge more for loans compared to their peers is limited. If loan rates are at 5.74%, Wells Fargo can earn 4.83%, which is the difference between 5.74% and 0.91% while other banks only earn 4.15%. This advantage makes Wells Fargo more competitive because the bank could lower its loan rates below those of its competitors, attracting more business than them and still making more money than them.

First Quarter 2009

When the economy was in a severe recession, the big banks were in serious trouble. During expansion periods, banks were in search of growth, and they relaxed their lending standards. They undercut each other, thinking that real estate values would continue to increase. During the most recent recession, banks lost money because they had bad loans on the books. As real estate values plunged, many homeowners had negative equity (outstanding mortgage amount exceeds the value of the house), which made them more likely to walk away and stop making their mortgage payments. As the situation worsened, banks were practically insolvent, and therefore, they were not in a position to lend, dragging the economy further into recession. The market feared that the government was going to nationalize or actually take over troubled banks, wiping out shareholders. The market was panicking so much that investors sold bank shares en masse, including the good ones like Wells Fargo. The price of Wells Fargo shares fell from a high of $44.70 in 2008 to $7.80 in the First Quarter 2009, which was a decline of over 80%.

Analysis

In 2008-09, Wells Fargo was not without trouble. On December 31, 2008, the bank acquired Wachovia with its horrendous loan portfolio. If Wells Fargo estimated the future of Wachovia loans incorrectly, it may cause them damage.

Despite the 2008-09 recession, Wells Fargo was one of the very few banks that continued lending. Deposits grew as people who wished to place their money in safe financial institutions switched to stronger banks such as Wells Fargo. With more deposits and less competition, Wells Fargo had the cash and found plenty of opportunities to lend. In addition, by acquiring Wachovia, Wells Fargo expanded its branch network into regions where it had not had a presence before.

Nationalizing a strong bank such as Wells Fargo would not make any sense. If the bank can weather the recession and not encounter serious problems with Wachovia's portfolio, the bank will come out of the crisis as a banking powerhouse.

Earnings per share of Wells Fargo were at $2.49 in 2006, $2.38 in 2007, and $0.83 in 2008. Based on the assumption that it takes Wells Fargo five years to recover to the same level as in 2007, the stock is worth over $28. Considering the strength of Wells Fargo and the acquisition of Wachovia, the bank can easily meet this assumption. At $10 per share, the stock is a screaming deal. Figure 47 below illustrates the valuation.

Fig. 47: Valuation of Wells Fargo

FACTS	VARIABLES		VALUE CALCULATIONS			
Current Trading Price	$10.00		Projected	Payout	Dividends	Discounted
Current Earnings Per Share	$0.83	Year	Earnings	Ratio		Dividends
Current P/E Ratio	12.0	1	$1.03	45%	$0.46	$0.42
Dividend Payout	45%	2	$1.27	45%	$0.57	$0.47
		3	$1.56	45%	$0.70	$0.53
ASSUMPTIONS		4	$1.93	45%	$0.87	$0.59
Earnings Growth Rate (1st Five Years)	23.50%	5	$2.38	45%	$1.07	$0.67
Earnings Growth Rate (2nd Five Years)	10.00%	6	$2.62	45%	$1.18	$0.67
Discount Rate	10.0%	7	$2.89	45%	$1.30	$0.67
P/E Ratio in 10 Years	15	8	$3.17	45%	$1.43	$0.67
		9	$3.49	45%	$1.57	$0.67
RESULTS		10	$3.84	45%	$1.73	$0.67
Value of Future Dividends Today	$6.01					$6.01
Value of Future Sales Price Today	$22.21					
Value of the Stock	$28.22	10	Projected	P/E Ratio in	Terminal	Discounted
			Earnings	10 Years	Value	Terminal Value
			$3.84	15	$57.61	$22.21
Discount to Value	64.56%					

In Figure 47, it is important to notice that the growth rate of earnings per share is 23.50% for the first five years. This rate was chosen so that earnings per share would come out to match our recovery assumption of $2.38 in Year 5. Similarly to

Thor Industries' valuation, Wells Fargo's valuation at over $28 is definitely on the low end. The bank could easily recover in less than five years.

Case Study #4 – Moody's Investors Services (MCO)

Moody's is a credit rating agency that has proved to be very profitable. Operating margins were over 50% each year from 1999 to 2007. Profit margins were above 25%. Earnings per share were $0.42 in 1998 and $2.50 in 2007, which represents an annual increase in earnings of 21.92%.

The Credit Rating Industry

The credit rating industry is characterized by a high demand satisfied by a few competing rating agencies. Two global players dominate the industry: Moody's Investors Service and Standard and Poor's Ratings. These two companies operate in a near duopoly. Together, they have 77% of the worldwide market share. They are in the business of predicting default probabilities of different kinds of debt securities and debt issues.

The first of two demand drivers for credit ratings is the issuers' desire to access global investors. Because investors rely on credit ratings to establish their required returns on investments, issuers must have their offerings (e.g. bonds, mortgage securities, etc.) rated by the rating agencies in order to access these investors. If the offering carries a favorable credit rating, investors will demand a lower interest rate on the borrower's cost of funds. If the offering carries no rating or a negative rating, investors might demand a higher interest rate or dismiss the investment altogether. (Fabian Dittrich. *The Credit Rating Industry Competition and Regulation*. Lulu. 2007.)

Risk-based regulation is the second demand driver for credit ratings because unrated securities cannot be sold to certain investors. For example, investment companies such as pension funds are required by law to hold only *investment grade* securities. In order for an investment to be considered investment grade, it has to be rated by a rating agency. By satisfying this requirement, the issuer obtains a "license" for accessing certain areas of the financial markets. (Dittrich 2007)

Competition in the credit rating industry is concentrated and is dominated by Moody's and Standards and Poor's. In addition to their reputations, the *two-rating norm* is a major contributor as to why these two companies dominate the industry. Over the years, the two-rating norm system was formed because two companies rated a majority of issues at the same time. The system is beneficial to investors because it provides a second opinion of default risk. Investors benefit from a second opinion, even if it does not provide additional information, because it gives them better assurance that the assessment of risk is correct. The two-rating norm system also reduces the probability of fraud. If only one agency was used, issuers could bribe the agency's management to obtain a favorable rating. Because two rating companies are used, there would be no benefit to bribing the management of one company, and bribing the management of two separate companies would be much more difficult. (Dittrich 2007)

Moat or Competitive Advantage

Moody's Investors Services enjoys a competitive advantage that comes from intangible assets, customer-switching costs, and network effects.

Intangible Assets: Reputation is the most valuable asset that an individual rating agency possesses. Because Moody's and S&P were the first to enter the industry, they had more time to build their reputations and brand names. Newer competitors are at a disadvantage. Even if it were possible for newer agencies to build the same level of reputation, this endeavor would cost them significantly more than it cost Moody's and S&P. Reputation is valuable because investors trust the most reputable agencies' assessments of risk. If issuers' goals are to obtain financing at the lowest cost possible, they are most likely to have their securities rated by the most reputable rating agencies. No issuer wants to buy a rating from an unknown rating agency, even if the price of the rating is significantly smaller because investors may not put as much credibility in that rating, and therefore, may ask for a higher credit risk premium when buying the investment instrument.

Moody's moat also stems from a regulatory advantage. In order for any company to enter the credit rating industry, it has to be granted the designation of "Nationally Recognized Statistical Ratings Organization." It is not easy to obtain this designation.

Customer-Switching Costs: High switching costs prevent issuers from switching from one rating agency to another. This is true only if the switch is in the direction from an agency with a higher reputation to an agency with a lower reputation. If this happens, it would create suspicion among investors who would automatically increase their *credit risk premium* to account for this new uncertainty. The cost of switching would be greater than the benefit of a cheaper rating. Also, investors could accuse the issuer of rate shopping, which is looking for the most favorable rating. However, switching from a less reputable agency to a more reputable agency would please investors; it would not create suspicions of rate shopping.

Network Effects: A network effect occurs when the value of a service increases as more people use it. Companies in the credit rating industry enjoy the benefit of a network effect, but the most established agencies, such as Moody's and S&P, benefit from it the most. Rating agencies assign certain credit ratings to securities by using *symbols* (Moody's–Aaa, Aa, Ba, Caa and S&P–AAA, AA, BB, CCC). These symbols are not standardized, which means that Moody's uses different symbols than Fitch or S&P. Investors want to be able to compare securities' risk levels, and it is easier to do this is if the symbols and scales are consistent. It would be impossible to compare a security rated by Moody's with some other security rated by an unknown agency that uses a different set of symbols. Therefore, as the number of securities and issues rated by Moody's and S&P increases, so does the issuers' willingness to hire them to rate new offerings.

First Quarter 2009

Moody's stock was trading as high as $76 in 2007 and had decreased to as low as $15.41 in First Quarter 2009. This was a decline of 80%. The last time Moody's was trading this low was in 2001. What happened? The housing bubble burst, and the country went into a deep recession. Banks facing huge losses decreased their lending. As the credit markets nearly froze, so did the demand for Moody's rating services. In addition, Moody's and other rating agencies were blamed for the failure to predict the meltdown and for giving the highest ratings to instruments that, in hindsight, were much riskier than indicated.

Analysis

Even though Moody's is a great company, it faces some uncertainties in the future. Because the company failed to predict the financial crisis, its most valuable asset—reputation—is in jeopardy. In addition, there may be numerous lawsuits targeted at the company by hurt investors. Because Moody's is extremely profitable, there is a high probability that it will stay in business and be fine in five to ten years following the 2008-09 recession. Moody's was not the only credit rating company that did not predict the crisis. Every other rating agency failed to predict it as well. Even if they had predicted the crisis and gave unfavorable ratings to many securities, they probably would have been criticized for being negative and hindering the economy from expanding.

As a result of the crisis, Moody's revenues and profits suffered. It might take several years for the company to recover, but because of its profitability and limited competition in the credit rating industry, the company will probably be able to grow and make money for years.

Based on the assumption that the company grows its earnings per share at 15% for the next 10 years, the stock is worth $48.05 (see Figure 48). In First Quarter 2009, it traded at $15.41 per share. This was equivalent to buying $1.00 for $0.32 or getting almost a 68% discount to value.

Fig. 48: Estimate of Moody's current value with 15% EPS growth

FACTS	VARIABLES	VALUE CALCULATIONS			
Current Trading Price	$15.41		Projected	Payout	Dividends	Discounted
Current Earnings Per Share	$1.85	Year	Earnings	Ratio		Dividends
Current P/E Ratio	8.3	1	$2.13	20%	$0.43	$0.39
Dividend Payout	20%	2	$2.45	20%	$0.49	$0.40
		3	$2.81	20%	$0.56	$0.42
ASSUMPTIONS		4	$3.24	20%	$0.65	$0.44
Earnings Growth Rate (1st Five Years)	15.00%	5	$3.72	20%	$0.74	$0.46
Earnings Growth Rate (2nd Five Years)	15.00%	6	$4.28	20%	$0.86	$0.48
Discount Rate	10.0%	7	$4.92	20%	$0.98	$0.51
P/E Ratio in 10 Years	15	8	$5.66	20%	$1.13	$0.53
		9	$6.51	20%	$1.30	$0.55
RESULTS		10	$7.48	20%	$1.50	$0.58
Value of Future Dividends Today	$4.76					$4.76
Value of Future Sales Price Today	$43.28					
Value of the Stock	$48.05	10	Projected	P/E Ratio in	Terminal	Discounted
			Earnings	10 Years	Value	Terminal Value
			$7.48	15	$112.26	$43.28
Discount to Value	67.93%					

If the company grows earnings per share at 10% over the next ten years, it is worth $31.45, which is equivalent to buying $1.00 for $0.49 or getting a 51% discount to value. This second set of calculations is shown in Figure 49.

Fig. 49: Estimate of Moody's current value with 10% EPS growth

FACTS	VARIABLES	VALUE CALCULATIONS			
Current Trading Price	$15.41		Projected	Payout	Dividends	Discounted
Current Earnings Per Share	$1.85	Year	Earnings	Ratio		Dividends
Current P/E Ratio	8.3	1	$2.04	20%	$0.41	$0.37
Dividend Payout	20%	2	$2.24	20%	$0.45	$0.37
		3	$2.46	20%	$0.49	$0.37
ASSUMPTIONS		4	$2.71	20%	$0.54	$0.37
Earnings Growth Rate (1st Five Years)	10.00%	5	$2.98	20%	$0.60	$0.37
Earnings Growth Rate (2nd Five Years)	10.00%	6	$3.28	20%	$0.66	$0.37
Discount Rate	10.0%	7	$3.61	20%	$0.72	$0.37
P/E Ratio in 10 Years	15	8	$3.97	20%	$0.79	$0.37
		9	$4.36	20%	$0.87	$0.37
RESULTS		10	$4.80	20%	$0.96	$0.37
Value of Future Dividends Today	$3.70					$3.70
Value of Future Sales Price Today	$27.75					
Value of the Stock	$31.45	10	Projected	P/E Ratio in	Terminal	Discounted
			Earnings	10 Years	Value	Terminal Value
			$4.80	15	$71.98	$27.75
Discount to Value	51.00%					

Historically, Moody's grew earnings at 21.92% annually from 1998 to 2007. The past is not a perfect indicator of the future, but given the company's strength, it should not have much difficulty growing 10% to 15% annually over the next 10 years. It might not grow at all for the first few years, but once the credit market recovers, growth might increase dramatically as demand recovers. Companies will always need to raise money, and therefore, there will always be a need for credit ratings. Moody's will be there to fill the demand for rating services.

Conclusion

In this chapter, four case studies were presented. All of them are excellent companies with moats. Because of the 2008-09 economic recession, their revenues and stock prices deteriorated. Investors willing to invest in these companies are likely to earn satisfactory investment returns over a five-year term.

Chapter 13

CONCLUSION

CONCLUSION

In this book, we learned that stocks are not simply ticker symbols moving across the TV or computer screen. They represent businesses. Great businesses with wide and durable moats or competitive advantages are able to earn high returns on capital, which, in turn, increases companies' earnings, making them more valuable year after year. If we purchase them at fair prices, they will make us wealthy over time.

To determine whether the price of their stocks is fair, we will value them. We will then make our purchasing decisions based on the valuation results. Once the market realizes the true value of the businesses we own, we will either hold them long term or sell them to finance the purchases of other great businesses.

We will have the fortitude to sell them when the market gets overexcited and overprices the stocks of our companies. When the next recession happens, we will not panic but will prepare for the stock shopping spree. When selecting individual companies, we will stick to ones that are not overleveraged because we prefer to own businesses that are so profitable that they can finance most of their operations and future growth through internally generated earnings.

We will not be searching for the next Microsoft in the IPO world because we know that the chances of getting good deals are slim.

And finally, we will not blindly over-diversify, preventing our individual picks from having meaningful impacts on the overall portfolio.

Performing the analysis presented in this book can present a challenge to some of us. It is not because we are not capable of comprehending the information, but because we do not dedicate the time necessary to research our investments. If our time limitations are such, we recognize that we need to find someone who has both the skills and the time to do the necessary due diligence. In selecting a professional, we need to be careful because the majority of advisors cannot help us. Unfortunately, many financial advisors are just out there for their own benefit, not for the benefit of their clients. These advisors are more concerned with their salesmanship skills and the quantity of assets under management than in delivering favorable investment returns for their clients. To bypass their lack of knowledge, they simply recommend broad diversification to protect us from their ignorance. This book will help us in choosing the right professional because it equips us with the knowledge to ask the right questions when interviewing the prospects.

Whether we chose to hire someone to invest on our behalf or simply to do it ourselves, which is highly recommended, this book is the foundation for a long-term investment success. We do not have to stay CLUELESS about the stock market anymore.

Appendix

REAL ESTATE OR STOCKS . . .
WHICH IS A BETTER INVESTMENT?

REAL ESTATE OR STOCKS ... WHICH IS A BETTER INVESTMENT?

Investors seem to be divided on the opinion of whether real estate or stocks are better investments. Whether we own stock in Coca-Cola or an apartment complex, we own a business. It is not important whether the vehicle to business ownership is a stock or a deed to a property, but whether the business has a moat or competitive advantage and whether the business was purchased at a low enough price to allow for favorable investment returns. When an investor loses money on a stock or real estate investment, he should not blame the vehicle to business ownership, but his inability to analyze the individual businesses.

We already know that some businesses such as Wells Fargo and Thor Industries possess moats, but can real estate have a moat? To answer this question, let's analyze this by examining the four sources of moats:

1) Intangible Assets

2) Switching Costs

3) Network Effects

4) Cost Advantages

Intangible Assets and Real Estate

Brands, patents, and regulatory licenses are sources of moats stemming from intangible assets. Real estate businesses definitely do not have any patent protection, but can they be protected by brands or regulatory licenses?

As much as some real estate investors would like to think that their house, condo, apartment complex, or office building has a name that attracts tenants, the reality is that in most cases, tenants are indifferent. They mainly base their decision on price, assuming the rental space and location is satisfactory to their needs. But in certain instances, properties can be protected by a brand name. For example, Trump Tower in New York City and Sears Tower in Chicago enjoy brand recognition. Owners of these properties can charge more than their competition because renting or owning at the Trump Tower or Sears Tower represents prestige and success. People will pay top dollar to be part of this association.

Real estate can also have a regulatory license protection. Every municipality in the United States has a planning and development department that regulates zoning for the properties located within its jurisdiction. A particular property may benefit from a favorable zoning classification that allows the property to be engaged in a more profitable operation, such as a nursing home instead of a regular apartment complex. The more difficult it is for the competing property owners to obtain a zoning change, the wider the moat of the property with the favorable zoning classification.

Switching Costs and Real Estate

It is safe to assume that all real estate businesses possess some type of switching costs. Tenants who switch properties have to go through the hassle of moving all their belongings. Apartment renters have less to move than retail, office, or industrial tenants. The latter have to move entire businesses, inform clients of their new location, and move the necessary equipment. Owners know the switching costs associated with renting real estate, and that is why many offer special rates at the beginning of the lease to get tenants in the door.

Readers should not think that they could not go wrong with real estate investing because the cost of switching will protect their investment. Moats or competitive advantages are there to protect revenues and profits from competitors. However, if all the competitors possess the same moats, there is no real advantage. The only way for real estate businesses to benefit from switching costs is to allow for the cost of switching from them to be higher than the cost of switching from the competing properties.

Two identical properties may enjoy different levels of switching costs, depending on the tenant mix. A sophisticated owner of one property may sign a lease with a tenant that requires the installation of heavy equipment. Moving such equipment to another property might cost a tenant a significant amount of money, which would make switching highly unlikely. Also, tenants such as dentists and doctors who spend money to build out their rental spaces are less likely to switch. If they go somewhere else, they will have to spend the money again unless the new landlord covers the expense.

Network Effects and Real Estate

As mentioned before, network effects occur when the value of a service or product increases when more people use it. Do tenants ever care whether other tenants are renting space at a particular property? Retail tenants do care, especially at shopping malls. These tenants want to rent space at the malls that attract popular retailers such as Macy's, JC Penney, and other large chain stores. Even smaller shopping centers attract tenants when Home Depot, Wal-Mart, or other big retailers anchor the property.

Rental homes, condos, and apartment complexes generally do not benefit from the network effect. However, there are exceptions. For example, senior housing complexes may benefit from a network effect because prospective residents will seek communities where there are opportunities to socialize.

Cost Advantages and Real Estate

Cost advantages allow companies to produce a product or provide a service more cheaply than its competitors. In real estate, this means the ability to operate a property with lower expenses than those of competing properties. Real estate businesses, just as any other businesses do, generate income and incur operating expenses to arrive at net income. In real estate terms, net income is referred to as *Net Operating Income* or NOI.

Income is derived mainly from rental income, but it can also be generated by other sources of revenue such as laundry, parking, storage, late fees, and application fees. Because cost advantages typically focus on the expense side, let us look at the expenses in more detail. Most property types have the following expenses:

- real estate taxes
- property insurance
- utilities
- marketing & promotion
- general & administrative
- management fees
- wages & payroll
- repairs & maintenance
- cleaning, painting & decorating
- capital reserves (money set aside for the replacement of items such as windows, roofs, HVAC systems, parking surfaces)
- interest on debt (not included in the calculation of Net Operating Income, but is considered a financial expense)

By reviewing some of the individual expense items, one may be able to find numerous opportunities for competitive advantages between competing properties. For example, owners of newer properties spend less on repairs and maintenance. Utilities also tend to cost less because newer mechanicals operate more efficiently than their older counterparts.

Older properties, on the other hand, have other advantages over newer properties. Real estate taxes tend to be lower because older properties have lower values and real estate taxes are levied based on value. Rents are also lower for older properties, making renting more affordable. The supply of older properties stays the same because it is impossible to build more 1970s-aged properties.

Larger properties have advantages over smaller properties. Individual condos and single-family homes have a hard time competing with larger apartment complexes based on costs. Large properties benefit from economies of scale because expenses can be spread among several apartment units.

Properties of the same age, size, and location can still have different advantages. For example, one property may be rehabilitated, and therefore, enjoy lower utilities expenses, repairs, and maintenance expenses.

One other important advantage that one property may have over another is the cost and size of debt. Most real estate, whether residential or commercial, is highly leveraged. Home and condo buyers may put down as little as 3% to 5% of the purchase price while the rest is financed by debt. Commercial real estate investors typically have to put down at least 20% of the purchase price. With so much leverage applied, the interest expense becomes the biggest expense item. Properties that are financed with debt that costs 5.5% have an advantage over properties financed with debt that costs 7.0%. Also, properties with less debt or no debt have an advantage over properties that are leveraged to the maximum.

Location, Location, Location

A location advantage does not fit into intangible assets, switching costs, network effects, and cost advantages; therefore, it needs its own category. A property's moat that results from location is the strongest and most durable moat. After all, a location cannot be easily duplicated. Houses, condos, or apartment complexes that are close to commuter rail or subway stations in New York City or Chicago can command higher rental rates than competing properties farther away. Retail properties on major thoroughfares or busy intersections command higher rental rates than competing properties. Industrial properties with rail access or proximity to major highways command higher rental rates than less favorably located properties.

Price and Real Estate

Now that we know that a particular property can possess a moat or competitive advantage over competing properties, we will examine price. Any investment's returns can be destroyed if an investor pays too much for the investment. The price is the aspect of privately owned real estate that makes it less advantageous than the stock market. It is very difficult to buy privately owned real estate at bargain prices. Usually there is only one seller and multiple buyers fighting over the property. In the stock market, pieces of the same business can be sold to thousands or millions of different investors. Private real estate owners know what they have, especially when the property has a moat, and they are unlikely to sell it for a bargain. Real estate is easy to understand, and it is more tangible than stocks. Stock owners may not understand the business or the value of what they have. There are many individual stock investors who never even read the annual and quarterly reports. Real estate investors, on the other hand, analyze the individual properties in great detail before purchasing them. Amazingly, when these same real estate investors are investing in stocks, they often fail to even look at the income statements and balance sheets of the companies they are acquiring. Thus, they are as clueless as most of the investors who also fail to perform due diligence.

Some might argue that it is not difficult to purchase real estate at bargain prices. If this is true, why are most buyers unwilling to purchase real estate with 100% cash? The reason is that if they did, they might only achieve a 7% to 9% return. To avoid this problem, they place a significant amount of debt on the property to increase returns to the mid- to high-teens, thus increasing the investment risk significantly. When the property's performance is in line with their projections, they achieve favorable returns. But when the property's performance fails to meet their expectations, real estate investors lose a significant amount or all of their equity because the losses are magnified by leverage. During 2008 and 2009, many real estate investors who purchased their properties at the peak of the market had to learn this lesson the hard way. When the economy declined, all of their equity, and in some cases their entire net worth, disappeared because the property values decreased significantly. Any investment that requires a significant amount of leverage to obtain favorable returns may not be such a good deal after all.

Stock investors were not immune to the downturn, but those who were not overleveraged did not lose everything. Whatever they had left, which in many cases was approximately 50% or slightly more, can still be invested. But for those who lost everything, future returns are not important because zero times anything is still zero.

Conclusion

It is a false assumption that investment in either real estate or stocks is the better investment. They both are simply vehicles to business ownership. Buying great businesses at favorable prices without risking too much is the name of the game. What gets investors into trouble is not the vehicle, but the fact that they acquire weak businesses at high prices and apply too much leverage to finance the acquisition. In other words, they unfortunately apply the following formula.

Weak Business + High Price + Lots of Leverage + Weak Economy = Investment Disaster

Printed in the United States
222218BV00004B/4/P

9 780615 287485